Racism

ALBERT MEMMI

Racism

FOREWORD BY

KWAME ANTHONY APPIAH

TRANSLATED AND

WITH AN INTRODUCTION

BY STEVE MARTINOT

UNIVERSITY OF MINNESOTA PRESS

MINNEAPOLIS / LONDON

First published in France as *Le Racisme,* copyright Editions Gallimard 1982; revised edition published in 1994.

"An Attempt at a Definition," by Albert Memmi, translated by Eleanor Levieux, is reprinted from *Dominated Man,* by Albert Memmi (New York: Orion Press, 1968), 185–95, and was originally published in *Le Nef* 19–20 (Paris, 1964); copyright Editions Gallimard, Paris, 1968. "What Is Racism?" by Albert Memmi, translated by Steve Martinot, was originally published in *L'Encyclopaedia Universalis* (1972). "The Relativity of Privilege," by Albert Memmi, translated by Howard Greenfield, is reprinted from *The Colonizer and the Colonized,* by Albert Memmi (Boston: Beacon Press, 1965), 10–17; copyright 1967 by Albert Memmi and used by permission of Viking Penguin, a division of Penguin Putnam Inc. "The Mythic Portrait of the Colonized," by Albert Memmi, translated by Howard Greenfield, is reprinted from *The Colonizer and the Colonized,* by Albert Memmi (Boston: Beacon Press, 1965), 79–91; copyright 1967 by Albert Memmi and used by permission of Viking Penguin, a division of Penguin Putnam Inc.

Published by the University of Minnesota Press
111 Third Avenue South, Suite 290
Minneapolis, MN 55401-2520
http://www.upress.umn.edu

Library of Congress Cataloging-in-Publication Data

Memmi, Albert.
[Racisme. English]
Racism / Albert Memmi ; foreword by Kwame Anthony Appiah ; translated and with an introd. by Steve Martinot.
p. cm.
Includes bibliographical references.
ISBN 0-8166-3164-6 (hc.) — ISBN 0-8166-3165-4 (pbk.)
1. Racism. 2. Discrimination.
HT1521.M4413 2000
305.8—dc21 99-047227

Printed in the United States of America on acid-free paper

The University of Minnesota is an equal-opportunity educator and employer.

11 10 09 08 07 06 05 04 03 02 01 00 10 9 8 7 6 5 4 3 2 1

CONTENTS

FOREWORD vii
Kwame Anthony Appiah

LIST OF WORKS BY ALBERT MEMMI xii

INTRODUCTION: THE DOUBLE CONSCIOUSNESS xv
Steve Martinot

DESCRIPTION 1

DEFINITION 89

TREATMENT 123

APPENDIX A: AN ATTEMPT AT A DEFINITION 169

APPENDIX B: WHAT IS RACISM? 183

APPENDIX C: THE RELATIVITY OF PRIVILEGE 197

APPENDIX D: THE MYTHIC PORTRAIT OF THE COLONIZED 205

NOTES 217

FOREWORD

Kwame Anthony Appiah

Albert Memmi is best known in the English-speaking world for his powerful complementary portraits of *The Colonizer and the Colonized,* essays in a tradition in Francophone letters of which Jean-Paul Sartre's *Anti-Semite and Jew* and Frantz Fanon's *Black Skin, White Masks* are the most distinguished predecessors. In this tradition, a political problem—anti-Semitism, racism, colonialism—is explored in part through the sketching of a philosophical-psychological portrait of representative actors in the social drama; ideal types, if you will, of the Anti-Semite, the Jew, the Negro, the Colonizer. Like Sartre and Fanon, Memmi seeks to understand the processes by which the inhumanity of a political order is kept in place by ordinary people driven by intelligible, if unappealing, desires: he reveals the rationality of colonialism as a system, even as he displays its cruelties. In the course of developing his account of colonialism, Memmi had to come to grips with racism: as a Tunisian Jew, he had experienced a colonial system in which French, Arab, and Jew were central political categories, racially conceived. The analysis he first proposed ("An Attempt at a Definition," reproduced here in Appendix A) was one in which racists assign a differential value to the members of racial groups, on the basis of "real or imaginary" differences between them, in order to rationalize the privileges of their own "race" or aggression against members of other races. This definition did not insist that the differences in question be biological—indeed, in his discussion, he insisted that (real or imaginary) cultural differences would in some cases do the work that was done, in others, by (real or imaginary) biological ones.

The obvious objection to such an account is that it covers too wide a range of cases: it would make some British attitudes toward the French (and, equally, alas, some French attitudes toward the British!) racist, since there is no doubt that in each country there are people who believe in the cultural superiority of their own culture and in their entitlement to better treatment in view of that superiority. If every claim of privilege based on real or imaginary cultural differences is a form of racism, then racism seems to lose its specificity in the general morass of ethnocentrism and xenophobia.

So Memmi went on to propose a narrower account, which insisted that racism, in particular, was the use of biological differences—once more real or imaginary—to ground "(social or physical) hostility and assault." (This definition, "What Is Racism?," is reprinted in Appendix B.) This definition also laid greater emphasis on the doctrinal basis of racist attitudes (their connection with biological theories of race, which he calls "raciology") while still pointing to the more general range of phenomena encompassed in his earlier definition, which he now called "ethnophobia."

Here, in this book, Memmi moves back from the narrow definition toward the broader one, in large measure because he wants to say that the scientific theories—the raciology—are just "a pretext or an alibi." People do not treat others badly because they believe the raciological theory; they develop the raciology in order to rationalize their ethnophobia. And, Memmi argues, ethnophobia is only one instance of an even more general phenomenon, which he now calls "heterophobia," which covers all forms of domination based on real or imaginary differences between groups: men and women, gays and straights, natives and immigrants, and so on.

It is his care in distinguishing these different ways of thinking about racism, and his placing of it within the wider realm of heterophobia, that is, in my view, the great contribution of Memmi's book. This translation should be an especially welcome addition to the literature on racism in English, in part because careful attempts at definition are surprisingly rare.[1] One of the great moral achievements of the postwar period is that racism has gradually come to be seen by more and more people as a pervasive feature of modern societies and as something to be condemned. This achievement is weakened, however, by the lack of a thoughtful consensus on the nature of the phenomenon. Memmi's work is an important contribution to the development of that necessary understanding.

But more than this, Memmi's project is not just the analysis of racism, not just a project of definition, but also an intervention in the politics of anti-racism, offering us not just a sense of what racism is but also some tools with which to combat it. His starting point here is the fact that heterophobia is "the most widely shared attitude in the world." He urges us, first, to be conscious of racism, in ourselves as in others: disarming our own racism is, he says, "the first step, the price to be paid in advance." Second, he urges that, just because heterophobia arises naturally through the psychosocial processes he has described, we must continually be educating people to resist it. And third, because racism has an institutional life, it requires an institutional (which is to say a political) response. In the work of self-criticism, and of antiracist education and politics, Memmi's work can be an important manual, a companion in what he calls the "infinite task" of the "struggle against racism" that is "the condition of our collective social health."

New York, June 1999

LIST OF WORKS BY ALBERT MEMMI

Throughout the text of Racism *and the Introduction, other published works by Albert Memmi are cited. Quotations and references are from the following editions.*

A Contre-courants, illustrated by Michel Ciardi (Paris: Nouvel Objet, 1993).

Agar, un roman (Paris: Corréa, 1955).

The Colonizer and the Colonized, translated by Howard Greenfield, with an introduction by Jean-Paul Sartre and an afterword by Susan Gilson Miller (Boston: Beacon Press, 1991). Originally published as *Portrait du colonisé, précédé de portrait du colonisateur,* with a preface by Jean-Paul Sartre (Paris: Corréa, 1957).

Dependence: A Sketch for a Portrait of the Dependent, translated by Philip A. Facey (Boston: Beacon Press, 1984). Originally published as *La dépendance: esquisse pour un portrait du dépendant* (Paris: Gallimard, 1979).

Dominated Man: Notes toward a Portrait (Boston: Beacon Press, 1969). Originally published as *L'Homme dominé* (Paris: Gallimard, 1968).

The Pillar of Salt, translated by Edouard Roditi (Chicago: J. P. O'Hara, 1955). Originally published as *La statue de sel,* with a preface by Albert Camus (Paris: Corréa, 1953).

Portrait of a Jew, translated by Elisabeth Abbott (New York: Orion Press, 1962). Originally published as *Portrait d'un Juif* (Paris: Gallimard, 1962).

The Scorpion; or, The Imaginary Confession, translated by Eleanor Levieux (New York: Grossman, 1971). Originally published as *Le Scorpion, ou la Confession imaginaire* (Paris: Gallimard, 1969).

INTRODUCTION: THE DOUBLE CONSCIOUSNESS

Steve Martinot

When, in 1949, Albert Memmi returned to his native Tunisia from Paris, where he had been studying, it was as if from exile, and with a great sense of disillusionment. Having graduated from French schools in Tunisia, he had expected France to fulfill some of the promises of high culture and civilization made by French colonialism. Instead, he encountered alienation, venality, and dehumanizing suspiciousness. Upon his return, he involved himself in the national liberation movements that sought to free North Africa from French colonialism. He became one of the leading members of a new generation of Francophone North African poets and novelists, and he helped found a journal called *Jeune Afrique* (Young Africa), for which he was the literary editor.[1]

But in Tunisia as well, the wounds and cultural dislocations engendered by colonialism had produced a labyrinth of distrust and alienation. In 1956, when Tunisia gained its independence from France, Memmi was asked to leave. Having studied in the French Lycée in Tunis, and in the Sorbonne in Paris, he was thought by many Tunisians to have become a French intellectual, which made him suspect in the wake of independence from France. In addition, he was Jewish, which many Tunisians felt did not fit with what they, from their Arab and Berber backgrounds, envisioned for an independent Tunisia. Neither French nor Arab, he had become a French intellectual who could not relate to France, and an Arab nationalist who was not Arab. He was the Mediterranean version of the Duboisian double consciousness.

In *The Souls of Black Folk,* W. E. B. Du Bois argues that, for African-Americans, white racism has produced a kind of double consciousness: "the sense of always looking at one's self through the eyes of others."[2] It involves the feeling that one's consciousness and one's world are always spoken for, narrativized before the fact, and appropriated by the surrounding white society. For African-Americans, this translates into the inability to be non-black in an America that rejects Blacks, or the refusal to be non-American in an America that refuses Black Americans. For Du Bois, the strength to withstand and survive these contradictions and their psychic violence was a true measure of heroism.

What stands on the other side of the racist coin is the privilege of never having to live this double consciousness on a daily basis. Whites in the United States, for instance, do not have to think about the disparity between what they (because white) experience as ordinary, and what others, beset by racial hierarchy, live in uncertainty and guardedness. Most White people do not consider themselves privileged, but the freedom from having to deal with gratuitous hostility, or suspicion, or subtle exclusion, remains the quintessential privilege. For White men, for instance, civil rights and democratic participation are culturally assumed; they become surprised (or even enraged) when these are called in question. For other groups, civil rights are not a social assumption but a continual problem, an arena of political struggle against discrimination. This disparity between the political and the cultural, between the problematic and the assumed, between the withheld and what goes without saying, renders dialogue on the issue well-nigh impossible; each side finds the other unhearing or incomprehensible.[3]

It is this fundamental disparity, its banal, social "il-logicality," that Memmi seeks to illuminate, and to resolve. He does so by understanding racism as a structure rather than an idea, a social relation rather than a feeling or a prejudice. For him, the structure of racism has four moments. First, there is an insistence on a difference, whether "real or imaginary." It can be somatic, cultural, religious, etc.; what counts is the discernment of its existence, rather than its nature or content. Racism will add what content it needs for its purposes. The second aspect is that a negative valuation is imposed upon those seen as differing, implying (by the act of imposition) a positive valuation for those imposing it. Third, this differential valuation, which renders the difference unignorable, is generalized to an entire group, which is then deprecated in turn. And fourth, the negative valuation imposed upon that group becomes the legitimization and justification for hostility and aggression. The inner purpose of this process is social benefit, self-valorization, and the creation of a sense of identity for the one through the denigration of the other. And as is evident, the generation and expression of hierarchy run through it from beginning to end. Memmi suggests that colonialism provides the archetype for this structure of domination because its aggression against a weaker society requires disparagement of the other to justify itself, to legitimize having appropriated others' land and homes, and having benefited from truncating others' lives and social dignity. Racism is indispensable to the colonialist mentality, to make its domination appear reasonable to itself.

An important corollary to this account is that racism is not going to be understood through its content, which it changes at will; it doesn't care about the nature of the difference it insists on, but only that the difference exists and can be used to denigrate the other who is seen as different. Memmi suggests that racism's tenacity relies on its opponents' attempts to reason with it, their naïve acceptance of its arguments at face value. They do not see that if a group is denigrated through a difference that is given special notice, the difference had been noticed for the purposes of denigration and not because it had an importance prior to that purpose.[4] The specifics don't matter—which is why the "one-drop rule" makes sense to Whites who define themselves as white through it. What counts is the form, the self-approbation that emerges from the assumptions and disguises inherent in any negative valuation of another group.

Memmi was born in 1920 in Tunis, in the Jewish quarter of a city that was culturally Arabic. Except for the difference in religion, the two peoples lived similar lives. The food, the language, and the rituals of public interaction on the street were essentially the same. At times, the Jewish "quarter" functioned as a domain for separating and excluding the Jews from the rest. At other times, it became again a "neighborhood" from which the Jews participated in the social and political life of the city. In Memmi's first novel, *The Pillar of Salt,* this interface with the Arab neighborhoods, as well as the insulation provided, are both given cultural value.

Before European colonization of North Africa, Berbers, Jews, and Arabs lived in relative coexistence, within fluctuating hierarchical relationships. When French colonialism arrived, its weight fell mainly upon the Arabs, since they had assumed hegemony in that tricultural milieu. Though the Jews suffered anti-Semitism from both sides (the French Christian and the Arab Islamic), they were ironically also accorded a minimal respect. The French reserved a certain consideration for the Jews because there were Jews in Europe, and the Jews were not Arab. The Moslems had a regard for the Jews because both groups were "people of the Book" for whom the sacred resided in a community of discourse centered around written texts and the law, rather than a reliance on Gospel.[5] But the Jews were also scorned and were in turn appropriated by each side for use against the other. When the Arabs sought to develop movements of resistance against European colonialism, or for national liberation, they made common cause with the Jews, who were native nationals like themselves, but when the Arab movement required something more than anti-colonialism to unite it, anti-Semitism was deployed to that effect. Similarly, the French courted the Jews in order to buttress and consolidate their colonial rule, but once that purpose had been served, the Jews were set up as a scapegoat to distract the Arabs from that same European rule.[6] None of this, of course, was substantially different from the way Jews had been used in Europe itself, from medieval times until the Second World War; it is what many had sought to escape by moving to places like North Africa.

When Memmi was born, all this was in place: a tripolar space crisscrossed by myriad political and racialized machinations. When he sought to make "sense" of it, it was not to render it "intelligible" conceptually, as an ideological system, but as a set of social relations. Yet what sense could there be? And where could he go that would not catch him in its partisan hostilities and twist his attempts at critical analysis into one form of complicity or another? In France, he found only a form of exile from home; in Tunisia, only a second form of exile. Ultimately, he settled in Paris. The cosmopolitanism of Paris, with its many urbane forms of anonymity, provided a "place" for him in the world. His "home" became his resistance itself to the racism that had driven him into redundant exiles. When he speaks in this book of the moments and events from which his critique of racism developed, it is as if he were describing the landmarks of his neighborhood.

His companions, with whom he shared this community, were other anti-racist and anti-colonialist thinkers of the time—in particular, Frantz Fanon and Jean-Paul Sartre. Philosophically, he had always been close to Sartre. Both recognized that one was always responsible for one's relations to others, because one always chose, regardless of given social constraints and traditions, how one was going to relate, and thus who one was going to be in relation to others. However, whereas Sartre became engrossed with the dialectics of the individual in history, Memmi turned instead to the individual's integration in the structures of daily life. And while he treasured his association with Fanon, Memmi disagreed with him on the question of violence and the restorative psychosocial value that Fanon saw in it. For Fanon, violence was necessary to purge oneself of the sense of inferiority acquired through the institutionalized denigration and torture to which colonialism and racism subjected its victims. Although Memmi agreed that something had to alleviate the oppression and exorcise one's necessary accommodations to it, he did not think that violence as such would do anything but invert the relation of domination; that is, it would not dismantle its structure. Having been on both sides of the colonial relation at different times, he was able to see both sides—not as separate interests, but as inseparable elements of a single relation that had to be dealt with as a whole. Despite their differences, these three thinkers formed a core of anti-colonialist thought in France and North Africa that had a profound effect on national liberation struggles throughout the world.

For Memmi, racism emerges from within human situations, rather than simply as the enforcement of an ideology, or the "natural" belief some people have concerning their "innate" superiority. What makes Memmi's approach to racism innovative (though similar approaches are to be found in writers such as James Baldwin or Ralph Ellison) is its unending integration of the biographical and the historical, the personal and the analytic. In this book, he tells parts of his own story at the same time that he sums up his researches and conclusions concerning the hierarchical structures that oppression relies on. Conversely, in his novels, which also tend to be autobiographical, his narrator will adopt an analytic voice, interpreting the scene while acting in it. In *The Pillar of Salt,* Memmi moves smoothly back and forth between these modes of consciousness (the narrative and the analytical); in *The Scorpion,* he actually disconnects them both in narrative space and in orthography (the novel's different voices are given in different typefaces).[7] In effect, in his writing, he reenacts the double consciousness he himself had had to live in the world.

For us, this combination of the personal and

the theoretical, the individual and the historical, is of great importance. Let's look at it from a slightly different angle. The relation of the personal to the historical is a dialogical relation, in the Bakhtinian sense that one's voice appears both within the historical and outside it as individual at the same time. Oppressive structures skew this dialogic relation. For instance, for Whites, the social categories of "Black," "Native American," "Latino," and so on, may seem quite natural. But should Whites ignore their historical constructedness (e.g., the notion of "native" originally acquires cultural meaning from colonial settlement and a colonial point of view that sets indigenous inhabitants aside as other), they would fall into a certain complicity with the white supremacy that defined itself as hegemonic through its naturalization of those social categories. In contradistinction, the people caught in being categorized, however much they may try to reappropriate it in order to reconstitute a sense of autonomy, nevertheless find themselves in a social structure that speaks for them and that drowns out their voice by doing so.[8] For both, the personal and the instituted are inseparable; for the latter, the personal gets buried under the institutional, whereas for the former, the instituted gets ignored through the immediacy of the personal.

Thus, for Whites, the ability to contest racism hinges on understanding how they are given hegemony by it through their whiteness. The historical, as instituted, would have to be included in order to understand whiteness as hegemony and not fall back into racism's own self-naturalization. And a critique of the personal would have to be included to the extent that whiteness generally blinds Whites to that hegemony and to how it dehumanizes them as well as others.

To concretize this a little more, let us consider the question of generalization. The concept of race pretends to provide knowledge about who a person is through a generalization that somehow connects somatic characteristics to temperament, culture, or social propensities. This is the case for those superiorized by it, as well as for those inferiorized. Most people accept the idea of "generalizing" others to be quite natural. If racist discourse defines what is to be noticed about a person as racial, it evaluates the person through the generalizations it attaches (concerning personality, capability, culture, and so on) as social meanings. In this way it "speaks for" those it oppresses. But people do not present themselves as general cases. Individuals only present themselves as individuals. A generalization about people cannot come from personal experience; it is nonempirical. It must come from a social source. To approach a person as exemplifying a general case is to have accepted that generalization in advance, prior to encounter. Ironically, generalization serves to obviate real encounter with others, because it substitutes the prior generalization for the person encountered. Similarly, a group characteristic, which may appear to be perceivable in a group, has to have first been deployed as a "characteristic" constitutive of a "group" to be noticed as such.

If the act of generalization exists only because

people do it, they do it only because it is socially given. That is, the personal and the institutional are the necessary conditions for each other. Police profiles that focus on African-Americans, and a White individual's apprehension of Black people as inherently criminal (thereby implying that Whites are not) are two sides of the same coin. Both reflect the social hierarchy that empowers the ability to generalize in the first place. That hierarchy is always in play. While the dominant can "disappear" the other behind imposed generalizations, the dominated cannot afford not to perceive the particular person encountered, if that person has greater social power. Ultimately, we would have to recognize that, in the United States, anti-racist Whites would require an inverted form of the Duboisian double consciousness in order to see who they are when seen through the eyes of those who have been disparaged and displaced by Whites, and to see who they might be if they could only break out of having been generalized by their own history as Whites.

For Memmi, to understand racism and to grasp one's complicity in the injustice of its social institutions, the elaboration of its structure is the necessary first step. This is the process of definition that he undertakes here. He defines racism three times in this book, reflecting the stages of his dialogue with the subject. In his first attempt, he focuses on personal prejudice; in the second, on the institutionalization of exclusion, second-class status, and segregation. Finally, the third addresses the social benefit that accrues to, and the sense of identity that emerges from, the disparagement of others, from the disallowance of identity (and autonomy) for the dominated. These three aspects (institutional exclusion, personal prejudice, and a sense of identity) all function together. Personal feelings of antipathy and prejudice are not the core of racism; they arise in defense of an identity and a sociality of dominance. Institutional exclusion is not its core; the institutional works only if enacted and obeyed continually and voluntarily by individuals who gain their name and identity from it (e.g., Whites). And identity is not its core, since that is dependent on the others it dominates and centered in them, though it socially excludes them in the same moment.

Ultimately, Memmi argues, racism as a social system relies on its ability to define. There is (1) the act of definition of the other, as the power of one group over the other; (2) the fact of defining as a dependence of the dominant on the other for social identity, and the inherent hostility engendered by that dependence; and (3) the content of the definition, which becomes the legitimation of the dominance relation. Memmi then adds his own process of critically defining and theorizing this structure, as a project to denaturalize it, to undermine its normativity. This book becomes a meditation on social definition itself, in the course of which Memmi seeks, by defining racism, to establish a certain power over it. Without its universality, racism becomes an object to be examined and no longer a destiny to be lived. In this sense, the book is an activist book.

But this will not be a surprise in the United

States: activism first brought Memmi a certain recognition in the United States in the 1960s. His seminal work, *The Colonizer and the Colonized*, was widely read at that time because it was one of the few works that addressed the question of colonialism and the colonialist mind, which both the civil rights and the anti-war movements were desperately trying to understand. These movements sought to fathom not only how a person could think that Jim Crow, or police brutality, or the invasion of another country to prevent it from decolonizing itself and gaining its national sovereignty, was good, but also how so many people could simply acquiesce so easily. In writing this present book in the mid-1980s, Memmi is constructing a bridge between that time when segregation and racism in the United States were most forcefully called in question, and the present, with its campaigns to dismantle affirmative action, to scapegoat the Latino immigrant, and to distend the prison-industrial complex, re-inculcating an ethics of revenge, retribution, and forced labor.

If Memmi becomes a builder of bridges, it is to show us what we have to work with to build a society free of racism.

Because racism resides deep in the heart of U.S. society, the translation of a work on it from a different cultural milieu presents certain problems. The metaphorics of any two languages will always differ. In this case, because the subject matter is a discursive (social) construct itself, the relation between its own discursivity and the metaphor structures used to articulate it will be quite intimate. Memmi gives his analysis conceptual coherence and integrity through a particular set of metaphors that, for the most part, pertain to judicial or court proceedings: *accusation, accuser, victim, plaidoyer, aggression, profit,* and others. (I have given this list in French, and with one exception the English cognates are immediately evident: *plaidoyer* is a plea or argument for the defense, a defense attorney's summation.) But significantly, this choice of terminology is not always appropriate for the United States.

In Memmi's exposition, racism is a charge, like a judicial accusation, levied against an other, who is metaphorically indicted for being in some manner (racially) different. It implies connotatively that the other has, in being different, somehow broken certain assumed rules, and is thus not a good person.[9] The essential nature of the indictment is that it devalues and disparages the one accused, so that its target suffers from it. The indictment, however, is unfounded and wholly unjust, and the accused is thus the victim of an injustice (of being accused and derogated). Yet its purpose is fulfilled by its mere existence, because a certain social benefit or privilege accrues to the accuser through the very status associated with accusation itself. In addition, the social benefit will often involve real material gain extracted from the process of victimization.

Since the indictment is unjust, the profits or social benefits obtained amount to ill-gotten gains. This fact constitutes a countercharge that anti-racism levies at the racist. In response, the racist defends himself or herself by falling back on the same concepts involved in the original indictment (its derogation of the other). Thus, the indictment (of the other as different) does double duty, first as a rationale for oppressing and victimizing another, and second as the substance of a defense, a *plaidoyer,* to justify and legitimize having done so. Accusation, accuser, and defendant all locate themselves in the discourse of the racist. This conflation of indictment and defense is one of the things that gives racism the aura of objective reality. If Memmi's description of this structure illuminates its real self-referentiality, it also reveals that, in this system, the victim has no place in court.

Though this metaphor structure serves its purpose well in French (and has a certain explanatory power when literalized, as here), certain political and cultural problems arise when it is transferred to the U.S. context. For instance, within his metaphorics, Memmi can make reference to "the racist" as the one who indicts, and who is put on the defense in turn, but this mode of reference would not have the same conceptual weight in the United States. Similarly, Memmi's reference to the "victim" of the racist accusation, while descriptively correct, does not harmonize well with certain political realities of anti-racism in this country.

In France, reference to *"le raciste"* in a third-person nominative mode, as to some unspecified person who speaks and behaves in a particular and obvious way, upholding certain ideas and attitudes, would call up a more or less familiar picture. But in the United States it would not really be as clear. This is a nation in which (having historically defined itself as a "white nation") white racism has been wholly generalized and integrated into the political, social, and cultural fabric. Though it may be invisible on an everyday level, it is acted out by White people simply through accepting themselves without question as white. What then would reference to "the racist" actually mean? For instance, a liberal White person who gives deference in an obsequious way to a Black person (in a supermarket checkout line, let's say) is manifesting a form of special attention that withholds ordinariness in its obsequiousness; it thus constitutes a noticing, a distancing, and an objectification that reproduce the structure of everyday racist exclusion. What remains unseen is the reservation of ordinariness for Whites. The classic icon is that old self-proclaimed credential, "Some of my best friends are Black." Its implicit derogations sink invisibly into the category of what "goes without saying." Thus, it would not harmonize with Memmi's metaphor of an "accusation," which assumes a sense of articulate and overt intention. In fact, Memmi's terminology would disguise the cultural generality of the phenomenon. The denials are the same, of course; Memmi opens his argument precisely with the denials. ("That's not me; I'm not racist. I'm just an ordinary member of society, nothing special.") But the category of "what goes without saying" is not a denial.

Even on the political plane, the terminology would be a problem, for the same reason. For instance, in the battle for civil rights, "the racist" would refer to those against whom political struggle is waged, whether it be a Bull Connor, a scornful anonymous White citizen, or an amorphous social or bureaucratic morass through which one had to wade. For Whites, "the racist" would be someone else, who might be making things difficult but who might also just be in the mind of those desiring civil rights. In other words, the term too often does not pin anyone down. In translating Memmi's use of *le raciste,* I change it according to context, unless it appears in a mode of argument that warrants such a singular reference.

Let's look at Memmi's use of the notion of "victim." It is true that all racism is an attempt to victimize others. During the civil rights movement, it was important to point out how Jim Crow and racism in general had victimized people—specifically, to emphasize that they had not done it to themselves. But the African-American, Chicano, and Native American movements (not to mention the women's movements) have all moved beyond the mere proclamation of victimization to modes of self-affirmation (e.g., through a reclamation of histories, symbolic representations, and so on, that had been effaced or stolen by systematic oppression). Today, it is recognized that to interiorize one's devaluation at racism's hands constitutes complicity with it. A victimology is now seen as a form of self-victimization. Though the structures of White racism continue to victimize, the modes and ethics of resistance dictate nonacquiescence to the status of victim. To leave this political dimension out of account would be to ignore the importance of resistance. Thus, while understanding the coherence of Memmi's use of that term in his metaphor structure, I have chosen to translate "the victim" in a variety of ways, depending on context, but always with an eye toward recognizing the importance of ongoing resistance.

Finally, I would point out that the juridical has played too central and literal a role in racialization in the United States to be metaphoric for racism. Race and whiteness emerged as social concepts in the seventeenth-century plantation colonies only after a long period of gestation that paralleled the development of slavery. The first chattel laborers had been English;[10] English and African bond-laborers generally made common cause in escaping until well after Bacon's Rebellion of 1676.[11] The initial difference between them was that English bond-laborers had contracts and Africans did not. After 1676, the colonial elite legislated a social separation between them through (1) anti-miscegenation laws that, in 1691, banned all forms of intimacy (suggesting it was too prevalent for the elite prior to that time); (2) harsher differences in punishments for running away; and (3) laws (in the 1690s) conscripting poor White farmers and laborers into a control stratum to guard against slave rebellions—namely, as vigilantes acting in the name of "white solidarity." ("Whiteness" as a social category rather than a descriptive term appears in the 1690s.[12]) Special mention should be made of a statute of 1662 that gave all offspring the servitude status of the mother. Though it violated cherished patriarchal principles, it was in consonance with the interests of wealth, and laid the basis for an eventual biologization of the English-African difference, through the motherhood function. But more to the point, social criminalization has always been at the center of racialization, from the colonial demonization of slave rebellion, through the passage of Jim Crow laws after Reconstruction, to the present unfolding of the prison-industrial complex. Thus, while I sometimes translate Memmi's metaphors directly, I do not seek to maintain the coherence of the metaphor structure that he uses.

One final aspect of Memmi's writing needs to be mentioned. Memmi often uses the masculine gender as the universal case. In French, the traditional terms "man" and "he" still function in that capacity. There have been some attempts by the feminist movements to modify French in order to attenuate the male or patriarchal bias of the language, just as there have been in English. But gender is much more strongly marked and explicit in French than it is in English. Thus, greater possibilities of deploying gender-neutral language exist in English than in French. Where questions of gender bias arise from within the language itself, it is important to note them.

Because the patriarchal bias in language has been contested in English, I have seen fit, where possible, to include it in the translation. Three cases of male-biased language can be distinguished in Memmi's text, toward which I adopt different strategies. First, where Memmi attributes or deploys the male gender in his discussion of racist thinking or behavior, I usually leave it as it is. I agree with him that patriarchal thinking is akin in structure to racism as he is presenting it, to which certain male-biased expressions then make veiled reference. In those instances where the reference to racist thinking should be recognized as including women as well, however, I have sought to neutralize the male bias of the reference. A second case arises in the philosophical use of the male gender as the universal case, in which the transformation to gender-neutral language does not disrupt the flow of Memmi's ideas. In those cases, I just make the modification. In the third case, translation into gender-neutral language would disrupt the flow of Memmi's ideas, perhaps because they are themselves too deeply or unquestioningly embedded in historically patriarchal terminology—for instance, in eighteenth-century discourses on Man. Here I have left the male-biased form, while noting it through diacritical means.

Racism

DESCRIPTION

THE DISCOURSE OF THE RACIST

There is a strange kind of tragic enigma associated with the problem of racism. No one, or almost no one, wishes to see themselves as racist; still, racism persists, real and tenacious. When one asks about it, even those who have shown themselves to be racist will deny it and politely excuse themselves: "Me, racist? Absolutely not! What an insult even to suggest such a thing!" Well, if racists don't exist, racist attitudes and modes of behavior do; everyone can find them . . . in someone else. Racist speech and ideas should appear annoying by now, and out of style. They have, after all, been refuted again and again by intelligent arguments of every kind. Their real meanings should be well understood, and even the racists persuaded. Yet racist discourse never seems to lack for repetition or representation, as if nothing had ever been said against it. Then of what are we really speaking, and of whom? What will we need to do to account for these contradictions and this deafness?[1]

Since the racist point of view is still extant, we will just have to go back and address it yet one more time, and once more refute it, before attempting to analyze how it is experienced and enacted, individually and collectively, as a phenomenon. Whatever a racist person will say or not say, whether it be idiotic or truthful, whether it be done in a fanatical or normal manner, one should listen carefully, since he is the one who brings the subject up and who hits out with it. Even if we have to delve deeply into what he says, convoluted though it may be,[2] will it not teach us more about the speaker than what he seeks to speak about? We hope that will be the case.

What do racist people say, or what lurks in the shadows of their discourse, perhaps even disavowed by them?

Let us note, first of all, that racism claims to be coherent, and even systematic. Ironically enough, in this regard at least, it might actually be right, since others agree that a racist *theory* does indeed exist. There are many writings, some fragmentary and others quite elaborate, through which racist authors, convinced that they purvey a truth to a welcoming public disposed to follow them, can be assessed as to their credibility and purpose. And there are everyday, garden-variety racists who are neither expert nor specialist, yet seem to know their lessons well, certainly better than one who is indifferent or indeed anti-racist. It is a preoccupation, one could say, even to the point of obsession. In private gatherings or on the street, on the bus or at work, he (or she) will speak of it to all who will listen. He[3] searches for those who feel as he does—and their agreement fills him with satisfaction. But he also searches for objections to which to respond with winning arguments. He gives opinions on books, articles, and information, which he voluntarily communicates for the edification of all. He moves smoothly into meditations on human nature and the destiny of civilization. Though what he says might be considered a scientific theory by some, it should nevertheless be called a kind of philosophy—a racist philosophy, if one chose to extend that term in such a manner. It is an overall vision and a will to persuade, whose end is to influence people and to bring about a new order.

What is this philosophy? For what does it argue, and what are its goals?

If one ignores the idiosyncrasies, the doctrinal and stylistically neurotic distinctions between different "theorists," this "philosophy" can be seen to ground itself on three principal arguments, which could be summarized as follows:

1. *Pure races* exist, each distinct from the others, implying that meaningful biological differences exist between groups and the individuals that compose them.
2. Pure races are *biologically superior to those that are not pure,* and this superiority brings with it as well a psychological, social, cultural, and spiritual superiority.

3. These multiple superiorities both *explain and legitimize the dominance and the privilege* of the superior groups.

What soon srikes one about this "philosophy" even at first glance is the fragile contingency of each proposition, the weakness of its reasoning, and the spuriousness of its conclusions.

The term *race* already involves us in a dilemma. Historically, it refers to animal breeding, born of technical concerns with respect to agricultural production. Darwin is involved, since artificial selection is a way of imagining natural selection. But purity can only be a question of convention, an outgrowth of the goals and methods of animal breeders themselves. Obviously, in veterinary practice, purity of breed in any absolute sense is irrelevant, as is the question of a return to past breeds (where, indeed, would one go?). On the contrary, breeding is done with an eye toward the future, the conversion of a chosen idea into reality. "Pure" races, then, are artificially designated varieties that humans deploy to accomplish certain tasks. Their primary aspects are their various relations to those tasks, and not to any concept of biological purity. The best "race" of horses is, in one respect, those that run the fastest, and in another respect, those that work the hardest. Physiologically quite dissimilar, the Normandy workhorse *(percheron)* and the thoroughbred racehorse *(pur-sang)* are both the best, each in its own context. But it is difficult to see what that means when applied to humans. Except in certain rare cases (royal incest, for instance), artificial human selection has never been accomplished. At no time has anyone attempted to engender a breed of people; at least, the attempt has never been effective or even accidentally accomplished. We know of a few groups whose isolation was such that little outside influence touched them. But the necessities of survival, or the exigencies of war, have generally consigned humanity to continual intermixing; in effect, far from being static, human groups have undergone continual modification. Even aristocratic families that sought to be endogamous were never beyond "bastardization," and even the most closely watched harems did not escape secret incursion. Supposing that purity may have actually been the case somewhere, it is not the general case for humanity. In truth, with the exception of chemistry, the very idea of *purity is either a metaphor, a prayer, or a fantasy,* the necessity for which is produced only by a certain human desire for perfection.

Does this mean that humans are not biologically different? Of course they are. The partisans of racism passionately follow up on any new scientific discovery that promises to support their position in that respect. Yet on this question, hasn't everything already been said? We repeatedly hear talk of renewed right-wing racist movements, but what is always striking about them is not their originality but their dusty decrepitude. The truth remains relatively simple: *pure races do not exist, but humans differ.*

No argument is necessary to demonstrate how humans are different; any European city street reveals it. In the department stores or in the subway, one encounters blondes, black-haired people, light and dark brunettes, some with hair slightly yellowish, others reddish. Eyes are blue, brown, green, hazel; the hair, the nose, the lips . . . what need is there to go on with this enumeration, even for a single town? Not to mention the rest of Europe, leaving other continents aside. Yet at the same time, it is evident that no specific type of individual, supposing one could be isolated, constitutes a social group distinct from others. Each biological feature is distributed at random among nations, ethnicities, and classes. Within any group, and from one group to another, one discovers an entire variety of human types, though admittedly in variable proportions. Or, to say this a different way, among all groups, the same features are assembled but to different extents. In effect, while people are diversely different, no one group can exclusively claim for itself a particular assortment of characteristics.

This doesn't mean that there may not be certain predominant configurations of characteristics in localized areas, but they are relative. Compared to Europeans, Africans on the whole have darker hair, skin, and eyes. But one has simply to look closely, either among the Europeans or the Africans, to see the diversity. Among Europeans, people of the Midi are, on the whole, darker in color than those of Nord; but what variety there is in a crowd in Provence![4] When crossing the African continent, one encounters an extraordinary range of colors—not simply "black people." Between Africans who are almost white and Africans who are completely black, one finds all intermediary shades—from the plump pallid shopkeepers of the Tunisian or Moroccan bazaars to the tall Masai people of Kenya, lanky and black as carbon, passing by way of the miniscule Pygmies.[5]

In addition, there exists what one could call a *spectral effect.* From one latitude or region to another, the predominance of features changes, but there is never a real break. As on a spectrum, from one group to the next, one sees all gradations, all nuances. Sometimes boundaries appear cleanly delineated. A gathering of Jews from the Maghreb,[6] Corsica, and Russia all together in a hall in Paris would seem recognizable. But what is being recognized? A race of Jews? A race of North Africans, Corsicans, or Russians? Or is it simply a manifestation of ethnic or sociocultural convergence that in assembly accentuates its relative differences from other French groups: differences of clothing, of speech, of demeanor, and so on? A gathering of Bretons, of Alsatians, or of Provençals would give the same impression.[7] Would one have to speak of a race of Bretonnes, an Alsatian or Provençal race? If one takes a closer look at the Jewish gathering, for example, one would discover all possible variations between those of Europe, North Africa, or the Middle East. And if each subgroup is examined separately, similar complexities will be discerned. In sum, *it is impossible to match any social group with a specific configuration of biological features.* It is our malicious or anxious indolence, our intellectual myopia, owing often to distance, that makes us generalize or conceptually homogenize "the Arabs," "the Chinese," "the Americans," where diversity and variation are the case. But then, to generalize people it is simply enough to characterize them as "not like us," "not from here"—that is, see them only with respect to us and not to their own being.

This does not mean that *cultural communities* don't exist. But one usually finds the same spectral effect in each one, and from one community to another. History and sociology both repudiate any simplistic biological notion. France, a rich and geographically accessible country, has had people come to it from every corner of the globe. Many have immigrated and successfully found a home here, despite efforts to the contrary by the native population: Saracens[8] in the Midi, Germans in the east and north, Vikings in the west, and so on. All these peoples have made their contribution to the common gene pool. Indeed, the Mediterranean countries in general have been perpetual melting pots. Spain and Portugal were occupied by the Moors for several centuries; the populations of Italy and Greece are the results of continual waves of people back and forth between the north and the south. Corsica has undergone, if I am not mistaken, seventeen invasions! And what is right in front of our very eyes here in France? The need for manpower in Europe brings as many if not more different people than all invasions put together—and with the blessings of government, if not always with that of the governed. In France, four and a half million foreigners have come from the Maghreb, from sub-Saharan Africa, from Yugoslavia, Portugal, Spain, and Italy; they arrive on top of former waves of migration from Poland, Russia, Germany, Armenia. And this doesn't even include internal migrations. Paris, it is said, contains few Parisians (but then, what is a Parisian?). In

Switzerland, there is now approximately one foreigner for every six of Swiss origin (but then again, what does "Swiss origin" mean?). The Federated German Republic attracted so many Turks that the German government had to start rejecting them. What is the United States today, or Canada? Are these countries not mosaics of peoples and cultures awaiting, perhaps, a longed-for amalgamation? What will Asia become after its recent upheavals? Can one seriously speak of one China? Of one India? Let us end this tiresome and obvious litany.

Clearly, a reassessment is needed. People prattle on in a racist manner and others listen to them. The monster, like a hydra, again and again rears its ugly head, and once more it must be cut off. A while ago, racism thought it had found a refuge in the discovery of human blood types; here, finally, was proof of undeniable distinctions. The problem was that it was meaningful only at the individual level. This new sanguine "identity card," like the fingerprint, created greater difficulties for racist "theory" than it resolved because it complicated the process of classification itself; no two individuals were strictly identical. The differences of blood undermined the notion of pure or distinct races, and even that of distinct social groups. All configurations of blood type are possible in any society or social subgroup—but there is not only the blood. An eminent opthalmologist friend informs me that the human iris is comparably individualized; research is now being conducted to see if its topographical differences can similarly be used as a mark of identity. The use of the voice to open doors electronically is already well known.[9]

Our fundamental conclusion remains intact: except for those rare or hypothetical cases in which absolute geographical or social isolation may have produced a singular biological type, *the biological nature of human beings is constituted, and continues to be constituted, through continual admixture [métissage].* Without insisting on the paradox, one could say that we are all of mixed origin.

The second proposition of the racist argument should fall of its own weight, since it rests on the preceding one, which has been shown to be untenable. If the idea of a pure race is dubious, then a racial superiority in the name of that purity makes no sense. But let's pursue it anyway, as if the argument had value. Suppose certain alleged races, with their alleged purity, were superior to others. (No racist can complain about not having been taken seriously here.)

We find ourselves in an embarrassing position. The facts are ambiguous and the reasoning incoherent. Why would a "pure" race be superior to an "impure" race? Why would biological purity be superior to impurity? What does biological superiority mean? And even if there were coherent responses to these questions, why would biological superiority imply other superiorities?

In fact, nothing suggests that the most homogeneous race, even if not absolutely pure, would be more highly favored, either by historical circumstances or in the pursuit of any project. Here and there, in folk memory, one does at times find allusion to a famous clan or tribe, chosen for greatness by destiny or by the gods. This theme of election, or of a chosen people, contrary to popular opinion, is not specific to the Jews. But also, it never reduces itself to just biology, neither for the Jews nor for any other people. The French wish to believe they are the most intelligent and bountiful people on earth, the Germans the most proper, the Italians the most artistic, and the Jews the closest to God. The meaning of each is always the same: we are the best! When this contains a biological element, it is always vague, at best symbolic, and often contradictory: Samson's long hair as a sign of virility, the heel of invincible Achilles as a sign of weakness.

The notion of purity gets even more dubious. Mythic heroes are usually mixed, half-divine and half-human. One often finds they were nurtured by animals. In truth, we swim in the fertile waters of a vast popular imagination, sometimes exercised out of nostalgia for an age of glory to oppose to the mediocrity of the present, and at others, in belated homage to a conqueror invoked to excuse one's own failings. After all, who does not desire a more worthy self-image? What becomes transparent in these myths is their goal of establishing the past as the standard by which the future is to be judged. We have been great; why will we not be so again some day? It will be enough to be worthy of it; the arrival or return of the Messiah depends on our own efforts and virtue. And one can find a place for biology in this: to reconstitute ourselves and our greatness, we must first undertake to fortify the body; the soul will follow. By proceeding systematically, we can build strong vigorous men who are six feet tall, indefatigable, and infinitely audacious. If, in addition, we dress them in feathered bonnets or caps like smokestacks, what a magnificent army we can make, as big as we like! Which warrior, which statesman has not dreamed of such a formidable and invincible cohort, a body of special pretorians, soldiers, guards, infantry troops, paratroopers by which he can impose his will and his law?

The Nazis only reappropriated this ancient politico-military dream. Their predecessors had been without recourse to biological selection techniques, and so fell back on the banality of the market, purchasing or hiring the most exceptional men and the most alluring, seductive women. But the Nazis, thinking that their biological methods were adequate, actually undertook to build human breeding grounds, or stud farms. Subjects of both sexes were selected, given special nourishment, education, and appropriate training. The experiment was not conclusive; but, in all fairness, it was also short-lived. The fantasy has not, however, been relinquished; today, one hears talk of cloning, using state of the art technology to produce standardized identical individuals, perfect copies multiplied to infinity. The obsession with both homogeneity and purity goes on. But the original question still remains: why would biologically homogeneous beings, both genetically controlled and pure, be superior? And above all, what kind of superiority are we talking about? A biological robot might be more efficient for certain jobs, but what kind of efficiency are we looking for? Do we want specialized robots, however superior, or real human beings who are more and more human, even at the price of a certain inadequacy? Is our ideal man or woman one of physical vigor or intellectual acuity? Of sensibility or functionality?

Besides, long before humans began experimenting with breeding, nature had already shown where it led. Those who have lived outside history, isolated from its upheavals and conflicts, from its drives for mixture and amalgamation, far from benefiting from their insularity, have become vitiated and withered like plants without sun. The Noble Savage, that utopian myth adopted by eighteenth-century thinkers, has nothing better to offer as its patrimony, neither biologically nor culturally. In rural areas, those most sheltered from the tumult of city life, people are known to be less resistant to disease than their urban counterparts. Endogamy has never been a certificate of health. The Jews are a case in point. A tenacious people that has prospered culturally over the centuries, their supposed endogamy is a false impression. What maintained the Jews was not their isolation but their turbulent history, which has made of them one of the most mixed peoples on earth. There are no anatomical traits common and peculiar to all Jews. Similarly, the Americans, a mixture of people from everywhere, are second to none for the beauty of their babies, the creativity of their intellectuals, the know-how of their technicians and their business executives. Thus, the lesson is obvious: if we would maintain our superiority, we must defeat purity and ensure adulteration by others.

But moving on, we find only more confused concepts. Is the notion of biological superiority a question of vigor and health, of coordination and skill, of elegance and charm? Let us suppose that some kind of biological superiority actually exists. What then would suggest that it would translate into a psychological or spiritual preeminence? Neither health nor beauty is necessarily accompanied by a complement of intelligence, noble sentiments, artistic talent, and evolved spirituality, like some magnificent, parti-colored train dragged along behind. If physical strength or physical charm had been a sure guarantee of success in social dealings, one would see more athletes and beauty queens as heads of state. Which is not to say that sports figures might be less intelligent (that would be a gratuitous deprecation). But the inverse correlation doesn't work either. Indeed, one could very much regret that thinkers, mystics, and aesthetes so often project an image of weakness and an indifference to physical beauty—but that is a different discussion. Psychological superiority is ultimately just a better functional adaptation to certain situations, which means that, there too, there are many different superiorities. So even supposing that biology had a real role to play, it would be just one factor out of many in a complex equation, with no reason to claim to be the determining factor. From whichever side we address the question, racism's biological arguments prove untenable. And now it becomes clear why its defenders, though dead set on demonstrating the virtue of their cause, change the subject so often—that is, become evasive. But their constant circulation from biology to psychology and on to other domains will save them no longer.

Finally we arrive at the third of the racist arguments, which already crumbles to dust because it rests on the other two, and they have evaporated. The concept of a pure race is dubious, biological superiority unwarranted, and other modes of superiority not derivable from it. Yet, as before, let us grant this final argument anyway, the better to see that it takes us nowhere. We again end up in the same quicksand: why should any assortment of physical or psychological attributes *merit* any social advantages? Why would a natural superiority, whatever that might be, give anyone a *right* to certain bonuses?

Social advantage can, of course, be socially allocated, or made a matter of social agreement, and sometimes it just happens by itself. Some people are inclined to favor vigor, youth, and beauty. But these are matters of fact, and the racist speaks of rights. One's physical being is not always a matter of indifference in a struggle for power, prestige, or wealth. Women are well aware of this, they who don't have masculine weapons at their disposal. As with some animals, some societies choose their leaders from among the strongest males, or the fastest, or those endowed with some unusual physical attribute. In a curious way, television has brought back this rather archaic procedure; since its advent, charm and sex have become greater factors in political campaigns. A squinty or hunchbacked candidate will probably have less chance of being elected. But it is neither a rule nor a necessity nor, above all, a moral imperative! If one reviews documentary films from early in this century, one is struck by the physical ugliness of politicians, their appearance as corpulent or sickly, the comic spectacle they make upon the screen. One needs no great historical insight to see that the biological argument is an alibi, a general way of turning things upside down. Some aristocratic families try to explain their social status as derived from biological sources. If not heaven, then nature appointed them to fulfill their particular social roles. But who does not see that the real matter in question is the legitimation of their privileges, for which appeal is made, after the fact, to some natural or celestial dispensation. How many dynasties have as their founder an adventurer, a conspiratorial minister, or a plain thief! How many empires trace their origins to the usurpation of an upstart! Biology may in truth get the credit, but only by default, with a modicum of historical amnesia and a concomitant suspension of morals. It only seems to be a solid basis because it is visible—and "natural."

The proof is that, in the absence of any real biological distinction, one can easily be invented. The blood of noble families is supposed to be blue, and that of the kings of France to cure abcesses. One might just as well adjudge redheaded people or albinos to be the premier examples of the species, predestined to lead the people, and at least their characteristics have the advantage of being real. But no one has ever dared to claim that a particular psychology is associated with redheadedness, or that this pigmentation comes with an invisible golden halo, signifying a preeminent soul or a sublime destiny.

Is there nothing left to support the fable? Yes, the question of merit remains. Naturally, people seek to put themselves in the best light and to get their just rewards, whether in material goods or by more subtle means. The racist desires exactly the opposite; he wants distinctions and advantages to be given by birth to those who simply declare themselves by decree to be the best. He champions privileges that are above all a priori, through some biological or spiritual definition. Yet merit is neither atemporal nor abstract, and it is especially not biological. Hannibal was blind in one eye; Julius Caesar was epileptic; Napoleon had ulcers and was of mediocre stature. All three possessed superior intelligence, but it was not their potential superiority that inspired people, it was their ability to act in the service of a collective enterprise. Merit either merits itself, or it is in reality a privilege.[10]

To recapitulate: There are no pure races, nor are there even homogeneous biological groups. Were there any, they would not be biologically superior. Were they biologically superior, they would not necessarily be superlatively endowed or culturally more advanced than others. Were they that, they would not have any God-given right to eat more than others, to be better housed, or to travel in better conditions. They could certainly decree such conditions for themselves, and impose them, but then neither justice nor equality would be found among them. In general, the opposite is the case: artists, creative people, and inventors usually eat very poorly. In short, *racist reasoning has no secure foundation, is incoherent in its development, and is unjustified in its conclusions.*

In other words, racism is a biologism carried to excess, and a self-indulgent elitism. The first makes for poor science, and the second dispenses with science altogether.

For the racist, however, there is an investment in biological continuity and individual heredity, but this reflects a nonevolution of the species that even the most indulgent science, one already partisan to this type of explanation, would only partially countenance, and then only with extreme prudence. Though the part played by biology should not be ignored or minimized, humans are as much the product of their particular history as they are of ancestral heritage. Family situation, education, cultural traditions, social context, individual and collective events, and even (why not?) climatic conditions all contribute to each person's physical appearance. The human is the product of a confluence of genetic inheritance and cultural heritage in the broadest sense. The supposed purity of the one and the concept of causality implicit in the other are abstractions that arise either from fallacious science or ideological mystification.

Ultimately, elitism has nothing to do with science. In fact, it has no need for it. If it does appeal to the human sciences, to biology, psychology, sociology, or history, it does so out of anxiety for its own respectability, its need for a seal of approval. Though it is always a choice, made either from passion or deliberation, it cannot admit to that for fear of losing all credibility. What it chooses is a conception of "Man" and of human relations in which conflict is valorized and glorified, and in which the triumph of the strongest is desired and blessed. Of course, it follows that convincing the losers of the ineluctability of their defeat will be of great utility. As such, all racism wishes to see itself as a preordained force, but it is in no case an ethical choice.

Truly, nothing sustains the racist discourse, neither reason nor morality.

Are we done with this yet? One would hope so, and we would like to say as much, but no such luck. Thinkers and critics desperately continue to demonstrate the inanity of racism, underlining the emptiness of its theories and the illegitimacy of its goals. Antiracist militants continue to exercise a wealth of dialectical ingenuity to combat its arguments and denounce the iniquity of its positions. Yet the record remains sadly discouraging. Far from disappearing, racism seems more alive than ever, like a pernicious weed whose roots one never quite succeeds in destroying. Though they wilt in one place, they spring up in another. Why are the efforts of science and of people of good will so impotent? There are, I think, two reasons for this failure.

The thinkers and militants rely on logic and reasoning because they believe they are dealing with an opposing logic and reasoning. But *racism is not simply of the order of reason*; its real meaning does not reside in its apparent coherence.[11] It is a discourse, at once both functional and naïve, that is called forth and maintained, in its essence and its goals, by something other than itself. To understand racism, one must address the real purposes at which it is aimed and from which it is born. In addition, *racism is not a theory; it is a pseudo-theory.* Let us have done with the indiscriminate use of this term. What we have before us is a mythic and rationalistic projection whose source lies within lived experience itself.

One final practical consideration: if one wishes to have an effect on an enterprise, it does not help to denounce its incoherence if it is already manifestly destitute of reason. One cannot really mock the philosophical pretensions of something that is inherently hostile to wisdom. In other words, a refutation of racism's formal arguments is wholly insufficient; one must strip bare the underlying system of emotions and convictions that structure its discourse and govern its conduct. The first task, then, is to describe its experiential structure and reveal the conscious mechanisms that issue from it, in order to set in motion a means of appropriate counteraction.

OBSERVATIONS

Racism Is a Lived Experience

We should not let pragmatic optimism lead us into illusion. It is easier to contest an argument than an emotion; it is much easier to refute a discourse than an experience. That racism finds its genesis and its nourishment in ordinary experience should not be reassuring. On the contrary, its opacity and tenacity are enhanced by the banality of its sources. Alarmed, I suppose, by the idea of racism actually having ordinary or everyday origins, some people have criticized me for the generality of my approach.[12] Yet I find I must go even further in reaffirming what I've said. All things considered, I remain convinced that the experience underlying racism is wholly common (in both senses of the word), which is all the more important because its primordiality enables it to weigh heavily on a person's sensibilities. The underlying experience to which I refer, inherent in the human condition (and perhaps that of animals as well) is that *each time one finds oneself in contact with an individual or group that is different and only poorly understood, one can react in a way that would signify a racism.*

This is a troubling if not discouraging statement. What response can then be given to racism? One can hear the sneering laughs now: why accuse anybody in particular if the evil is so widespread? Are we then all racist for all times? No, not exactly. But we are all tempted by racism, yes. There is in us a soil prepared to receive and germinate its seeds the minute we let down our guard. We risk behaving in a racist manner each time we believe ourselves threatened in our privileges, in our well-being, or in our security. We conduct ourselves like racists when we try to reconstruct a state of parity that we believe has been or might soon be lost. If these situations arise often, racism assuredly becomes one of the most ordinary responses. And the onus rests on us not to succumb, to exorcise the fear, to analyze what is most often an illusory danger, and to defend ourselves by means other than a destructive confabulation or mythification of the other. Conversely, one gains nothing by closing one's eyes to this aspect of human reality. On the contrary, only by being fully cognizant of it can we hope to succeed.

Until the end of my adolescence, I lived in a country dominated by a social climate of extreme and reciprocal distrust, to say the least, between peoples otherwise reputed to be among the friendliest on earth, in a region that itself fostered calm and natural human interaction. Those who lived there, however, belonged to different religions, had different languages and mores, and lived in terms of more or less different, even opposed, interests. The result, despite the many positive sentiments naturally born of long social proximity, was a situation of mutual resentment, suspicion, fear, and hostility that manifested itself in every gesture and every phrase—and that broke out from time to time in social paroxysms from which the weakest and most poorly armed suffered the most. Later, when I traveled to France and Europe, I found little there to disabuse me of what I had already angrily learned. Of course, Europe's own ongoing mutual hostilities were somewhat pleasantly attentuated by its more homogeneous populations, its more egalitarian laws, and its longer traditions of democracy—all of which marked a certain degree of progress. But there was a suspicious and sardonic contempt for every stranger, a well-fortified reserve toward others, a practically nonexistent hospitality, a taste for secrecy, a systematic masking of one's activities, of covering one's tracks even to the point of having no signs on the house doors or information in the phone books (which often rendered them useless)—in short, an ingrained chauvinism, revealing a latent and aggressive fear of the other that manifested itself in gratuitous attacks on the street, in sports competition, or in songs. Legal or moral prohibitions had only to relax slightly, or economic difficulties to intensify, or international threats to appear on the horizon, for the beast hidden in each person to rear its ugly head and start going through its usual criminal gestures, namely, the silent treatment, the ostracism, the rabble-rousing, the mobs with a blood thirst, and the destruction of symbolic objects or places. During the Second World War, spontaneous hostility even broke out against French refugees themselves; the miserable people from Alsace-Lorraine[13] were charged with having once again sold out to the Germans, as were the Parisians fleeing to the Midi. Residing for many years in France, I often observed the quivering suspicion toward the Gypsies, the condescending hostility against immigrant workers, anti-Arab racism with its recurrent moments of violence and murder, the periodic reawakening of anti-Semitism with the burning of synagogues and desecration of cemeteries. One recalls the famous "rumor of Orleans," that astonishing accusation of gang rape supposedly organized by Jewish merchants against customers they had themselves chloroformed.[14] No small number of bomb threats occurred against Jewish institutions and student houses.[15]

Naturally, I'm not speaking of all French people; I am not going to fall into generalizations and stereotypes of my own. What I am saying is that every group, class, and ethnicity has its quota of those who think in a racist manner. Even on the left, there is a history of anti-Semitism. Recall the words of Toussenel: "Anti-Semitism is the socialism of fools." Fools or not, there are people who see themselves as both socialist and anti-Semitic.[16] This must be accounted for, especially when one is a victim of it. Moreover, it is not true just of France; no country in Europe is free of these same nightmares. England had the reputation for being the land of refuge, of sanctuary, but the immigrants had only to be exotic, and in sufficient numbers, for the same old social obsession to seize the English. Hindus and Africans have been chased down the streets of London. Where in the world does this pernicious flame not burn, in need of being extinguished? Must we recall the extraordinary visceral and irrational hatred of Black people in North America, the apartheid of South Africa, the interethnic aversions among the Brazilians, the anti-Semitism of Argentina? The communist countries decided not to name this vile evil in order to pretend that they were clean. Racism is outlawed by their constitutions—that was sufficient for people to think of it!

Such things are, I repeat, an aspect of collective life. There are also positive and sustaining dimensions to social reality, since a collective life is possible. All social affairs presuppose a *reciprocal dependence*[17] between their participants. But fear, hostility, and aggression are also aspects of human interactions. With regard to the other, each one of us is capable of both positive and negative reactions. In that sense, *racism manifests a failure of relations with the other.* But it is a failure that has become, in some sense, conventional. Ask people at random what they feel upon encounter with a foreigner. First, there is mistrust, if not repulsion and fear. The foreigner is like an unfamiliar plant growing by the side of the road, whose odor itself may be noxious. A stranger's mere appearance, when he approaches, becomes a provocation and sets one on edge, put more on the defensive the closer he gets. An encounter with Martians, however inoffensive they might be, would produce fear and panic. Everything happens as if, in the midst of being attracted and curious, there is also the onset of an allergic reaction to the other. Indeed, the word "allergy" derives from *allas,* the Greek for "other," and *ergon,* which means reaction.

Undeniably, difference is disquieting; it reflects the unknown, and the unknown often seems full of danger. Difference disturbs even when, at times, it seduces. Seduction and a sense of apprehension do not contradict each other. They belong to that agreeable curiosity that produces an attraction toward the unknown, a taste for the exotic, for voyages, for cultural and commercial adventures. The sense of "disquieting strangeness" is an intimate ingredient of the excitement. As it is said, shadow accompanies all light.

For example, it is usually assumed that parental or romantic relations are the purest and most humanly affirmative of our existence. But nothing could be further from the truth! Images of children put to death are all too familiar. The titan Cronus devoured his own children; Agamemnon sacrificed his daughter by fire in exchange for favorable winds; Abraham consented to sacrifice his son by the knife, which was stopped only at the last minute by divine intervention; the first born were exterminated in Egypt, not to mention the thousands of small burned skeletons in Phoenician tombs, a testament that the appetite of Baal was not a myth without consequences. Finally, was not Christ a son given in sacrifice? And why not recognize that we ourselves send our young men to death whenever "the nation is in danger"?

Love is not exempt from cruelty either. Unquestionably, male fantasies about women lead often to aggression against them, and even to murder. Dreams, hospitals, and all kinds of works of art are full of violated women, bloodied women, women who have been maimed and massacred. The principal interest of the awful Marquis de Sade is the blatant revelation of these shameful secrets. The willful violence against women arises without doubt from the dread men feel in facing them. At the same time, the love relation is one of the richest and most self-affirming. Yet men hardly know women; they misunderstand women because women are different from them. Biologically, a woman is already foreign to men, perhaps even somehow monstrous, with protuberances on her chest and a hole at the base of her abdomen where the sex organ should be. A familiar and attractive monster, perhaps, fascinating at times in the way cats are, but always strange. The deflowering of a woman is a violent and transformative act. Aside from pleasure, many men come to feel a sense of guilt about it, which feeds the natural aggressiveness that is, in turn, indispensable to accomplishing something required for species survival. And a man's relation to a woman is not simply limited to her femaleness. Each man has had a mother. Motherhood is not subsumed just by its nurturing role; the mother is a formidable presence as well, awesome in effects that go well beyond the child's upbringing. Fear and resentment, there too, are not far away. (Having just finished writing these lines, I perceive, to my dismay and shame, that I have described the man-woman relation only from the point of view of the man! Q.E.D. Of course, this picture must be completed by presenting the other perspective: how women live the anatomical differences, the threat of violation that is always on a woman's horizon, and so on.)

Naturally, all this is not exactly about racism. Racism only begins with an interpretation of differences, from which arise both the dreams and invented narratives of the other and, at times, the attacks. If the interpretation is positive, or the dream agreeable, then there is no aggression. *But whether agreeable or disagreeable, difference, it must be acknowledged, is never neutral.*

A short time ago, the mayor of a resort town attempted to prohibit the use of the beach to the mentally handicapped, explaining that otherwise many other vacationers might leave. This justifiably caused considerable scandal; he did not have the right to exclude any category of people from enjoying the sun or the sea. But though he was morally wrong, this honorable official expressed a very common sentiment: physical or psychological differences, bodily or mental dysfunction, can create extreme anxiety, even among professional caregivers and specialized educators—even if they refuse to acknowledge it. This reality can be confirmed with a small experiment. Dangle a spool from an invisible nylon thread in the air in front of a dog; the animal, whose eyesight is not particularly sharp, will show visible disquiet in the face of this unknown phenomenon.

Racism as a Common and Socialized Experience

If racism is first of all a lived experience, it is also a social experience that is very widely shared. This is a necessary precondition for its use as a conceptual machine by which to destroy other people. Colonists are usually racist, yes, but the colonized are also. No Manicheanism is possible here. The sin is committed even by its victims, on their own. The colonial settler, the lower-class White, or the European national with only a mediocre upbringing have no need to read Gobineau or *Mein Kampf* to despise the indigenous, or the Jew, or the immigrant. The colonized, or those who belong to a minority, have no need of reference books to become xenophobic, and their own traditional texts probably even counsel respect for strangers.

It is easy to discern the faults of others, above all if they have also made the mistake of being powerful, formidable, and privileged. It is harder to accept it in oneself and one's own people, above all if they are themselves victims. Why add to their misery? Nevertheless, it should be done if the awareness it produced were to lead to a remedy, if it exists. Among Whites, Blacks, Asians, Arabs, Jews, Indians, members of African clans, Asiatic tribes, and other diverse communities, there are forms of racism. It is found all around us; at birth, we imbibe it with our mother's milk. It comes to us with our first words. The disquisitions and arguments, the explanations and refutations come later, to give form to the deleterious clouds that already surround us. In Tunisia, there are French, Italians, Maltese, Greeks, Spanish, Turks, Russians, and Moslem and Jewish Tunisians, and each group has its racists, who are more or less open about it. To varying degrees, each of us, in our own way, with diverse and often contradictory arguments, has held all others in suspicion, rejecting and condemning them in advance, just because they were them, and we were us. It was all common and reciprocal, committed from impotence and the desire for power.

The European colonists, as the dominant group, literally had to be racist to legitimize their control. To continue to live as colonists, to which all alternative had already become unimaginable for them, they had to render inferior their ill-fated partners in the colonial relation.[18] But they did it out of fear as well, that fear which besets any controlling minority, even when protected by the police and the army and comforted by close connections to a colonial homeland. The racism of White South Africans contains these two elements: self-justification through persecution of the other, the native South Africans, and a flight from fear of the other through self-affirmation. But the colonized themselves have their own racism, not so much against the Europeans, who fascinate them, but against other groups more vulnerable than themselves, over whom they can exercise a compensatory power in turn. The Jews, for example, have done this out of a need to respond in kind, to avenge themselves for their thankless lot. And then there are the Sicilians, the Maltese . . .

In other words, in considering so common a phenomenon, one can say that *racism only becomes racism within a social context.* Later, we will elucidate its general mechanisms as a behavior of refusal. But for the moment, we wish to consider what lies beyond pure emotion and beyond the pure concepts that result from abstract analysis. As concretely experienced, racism is a real though destructive relation between two individuals who emerge from their own particular socially given contexts. Though racism generates a totally negative vision of the other, who is then seen grossly distorted behind the mists of prejudice, it is nevertheless an experience of the other, a complex experience in its own problematic way. But it remains a conflict between two modes of membership in social contexts that provide the mediations and generalizations, the images and arguments that sustain and valorize its alibis and myths. In sum, *racism is a cultural, social, and historical presupposition.*

In my own case, I first encountered racism in the context of colonialism. In a way, I was lucky (in the sense that one might speak of a nice scar, or the visibility of a tumor whose growth allows one to better diagnose its nature). At every step, I saw racism in operation, blatantly and without disguise. One had very little choice. Those early experiences remain unchallenged and fundamental to all my later reflections. The hero of my first book, a novel *(The Pillar of Salt)*, encounters racism and xenophobia from childhood on, in the streets, in school and other government institutions, in the newspapers, and in social organizations. The story is awash in their diffuse currents, punctuated by scenes of sudden violence. Later, I sought to be more reflective in my writing, in order to analyze and elucidate these general and recurrent phenomena.

Racism and Colonization

Perhaps I focus too much, however unconsciously, on the genesis of racist thinking. If I truly believe that one's lived experience is the touchstone that both filters and safeguards one's thinking as it circulates between its points of departure and its ultimate results, it is because I also think there is no substitute for sensitivity in one's apprehension of reality. Truly, a rational ordering of things is essential. Yet in spite of having lived with racism daily, in the grocery store, on the way to school, in high school, it took a profoundly disruptive historical crisis to shake me out of the realm of personal experience and push me toward an attempt to explicate its general mechanisms. Still, mine was only one particular experience, in one particular country—and I have been criticized on that score with respect to my first analyses of colonialism. But I don't see any contradiction. There are only particular cases, which it is necessary to articulate, to compare, and to compile through more general interpretations. Let us simply say that all experience is particular, but that science and knowledge begin with comparison.

In any case, to return to Tunisia at the beginning of the events that would ultimately bring independence to that country was to be thrown into a profoundly traumatic situation. I had connections and friendships in both camps. Colonizers and colonized are not simply theoretical or abstract figures; they are real men and women, parents, colleagues—and myself!—whom I moved along with in the currents of daily life. I found myself with the insatiable need to understand, if not to approve, both sides. I decided to paint a double portrait, as faithful as possible to each. The result was the book *The Colonizer and the Colonized*. It set in relief, among other things, the points at which we were tied one to the other, in the sense that the attributes and behavior of each were reflected in the other. My main point was that one colonial relation existed, in which everyone was necessarily implicated. And I discovered, in the course of methodical analysis, that racism was one of the inevitable dimensions of this relation.

I admit to having to erase all local color, the specificity of the psychological landscape, in order to trace the structural outlines of colonization. And racism undeniably constituted part of even the most simplified drawing. No doubt, whether in the colony or elsewhere, racist thinking is not limited simply to the colonialist. I have elsewhere sought to describe, in a somewhat less rigorous manner, the racism found among other peoples. But the racism of Arabs, Jews, or Maltese is not essentially linked to the colonial relation. It has other sources, to which I will return later. All I'm saying is that the colonizer *as such* is almost always racist. This is not the place to recall certain distinctions I have made between different categories of colonizers and the good will evinced by some of them. I would instead reaffirm that there really does not exist a colonial relation in which racism is not only present but intimately linked to that relation. It seems to me justified to conclude that *racism illustrates, summarizes, and symbolizes the colonial relation.*

In *The Colonizer and the Colonized,* I proposed an analysis of three major points: (1) racism, first of all, puts in relief certain differences; (2) it bestows a value on those differences; and (3) it utilizes the valuation of those differences to the benefit of one noticing them and giving them a value. What I noted as well is that no one of these conditions, by itself, is sufficient to constitute racism. Much misunderstanding, along with useless guilt, in a domain already rich in that, would be avoided if one kept in mind their necessary conjunction.

To insist on a difference, biological or otherwise, is not racism, even if it is a dubious difference. To put a difference in relief, to point it out to be noticed, when it does not exist, is not a crime; it is either an error or an insult. To call attention to a difference, when it does exist, is still less blameworthy. One even has the right to believe that it is legitimate to do so; after all, curiosity is the first step toward knowledge. The examination of differences between people is the very object of anthropological science. In fact, that discipline is divided into biological anthropology and social anthropology; thus, it embodies in itself the difference between biological difference and cultural difference. Psychology and sociology proceed similarly, though through the study of resemblances as well as of differences. It would not be useful to suspect all researchers in the human sciences of racism. *The description of a difference does not constitute racism; it constitutes a description.* However, it must be noted that such descriptions can be used by racism in its attacks. But a differential trait by itself does not justify prejudicial hostility; on the contrary, it only takes on that kind of phantasmic significance when it is placed in a racist discourse.

Second, to put a value on a difference to one's advantage is also insufficient to denote a racist mentality. The valorization of difference is, in fact, a common tendency—though usually unjustified and thus a trifle vain. The mistake that is usually made lies in considering difference out of context; wrongly contextualized, it augments a sense of anticipation or disquiet, which contributes to the preferences one might have for those who share one's own appearance and customs. A friend recently returned from a trip to sub-Saharan Africa. He told me of being surprised and disturbed by some of the inhabitants' behavior, which was totally incomprehensible to him. Fortunately, he is a scrupulous man and somewhat skeptical with respect to himself. He decided that two hypotheses were possible: either these people were of another "race," implicitly inferior, or he did not know how to interpret their behavior because he lacked sufficient information concerning the whole of their traditions and their life. The first interpretation lies in the category of racism, because it would inferiorize the Africans to the advantage of Whites; the second one doesn't. In both, there is astonishment and a sense of strangeness, but in the last analysis, there is also the right of all people to live in their own particular manner simply because it is familiar. One has the right to prefer brown eyes over blue, straight hair over tightly curled, one form of nose to another. It would be a bad argument, one lost in advance (if not a source of hypocrisy), to attempt to impose an aesthetic or erotic norm. That would constitute a form of inverted racism.[19] Rather, we bring our own patterns with us from childhood that reflect those first beings who leaned over our cradle: father, mother, and other family members. There is no doubt that our earliest experiences have a decisive influence on our tastes, on what attracts and repels us. Yet even those are not simplistic or even direct influences. Some men prefer blondes out of fidelity to their mother, while others prefer brunettes in opposition to the blondness of their mother; the son of a Catholic family might become a communist or freemason as a counterbalancing reaction to paternal influence. There is nothing remarkable or problematic about this. And none of it need be a source of guilt, though it might be useful in bringing certain psychological aspects of oneself to light.

Ultimately, one becomes racist only with the inclusion of the third point: the deployment of a difference to denigrate the other, to the end of gaining privilege or benefit through that stigmatization. To claim, rightly or wrongly, that a colonized people is technologically inferior to another is not yet racism: it is something to be discussed and either affirmed or refuted. But colonialism does not content itself with merely making such a statement and possibly being mistaken; it goes on to conclude that it not only can but should dominate the colonized. And that is what it has done. Colonialists have always explained and justified their presence in the colony by the poverty and backwardness of the colonized. And they have also been convinced that the colonized should thank them for having taken the trouble to devote themselves to the well-being of such poor inferior people! Indeed, had it not been for the stakes involved, would not colonization have truly been considered a philanthropic enterprise? But it was, above all, a system of rapacious depredation.

These three major points of the racist argument, then, form a whole. Moreover, as an argument, they must be interpreted as a whole whose function is revealed by where it leads, and by what then signifies its inherent orientation. In the repertoire of colonialist activity, one thing is blindingly clear: the entire machinery of racism, which is nourished on corruption, whether shameless and blatant or whispered and allusive, and which produces a vast lexicon of official words, gestures, administrative texts, and political conduct, has but one undeniable goal: the legitimization and consolidation of power and privilege for the colonizers.

INTERPRETATION

Racism and Difference

The fact remains that *difference is the principal notion around which the racist enterprise revolves.*[20] The idea of difference has become quite fashionable today; the banner of the "right to difference" has been raised by many revindicating social struggles. But this has not simplified things; within the swelling ranks of its proponents, there are those who sometimes go to foolish extremes. Similarly, in advertising campaigns, one finds such slogans as "taste the difference," or a product that offers "more than difference." Difference is made to be a quality in and of itself, the essential property of a mineral water or a car, the meaning of its carbonation or of some accessory gadget. This becomes a serious matter when, and with all due respect, certain retrograde practices become glorified as "ethnic" under the guise of the "right to difference," though they are actually quite harmful: female genital mutilation, for instance, or certain unhealthy practices of magic.

But do we really have to choose between a "differentialism" that extols all within a cultural tradition as good and worthy of protection on the one hand, and a condemnation of all particularism on the other?[21] Having been one of those responsible for promoting the question of difference (see my *Portrait of a Jew*), I would like to address a certain misunderstanding that has become attached to it. In reviewing the issue, I recall that it is not so much difference itself that is important as the significance given to it.

Not to keep this in mind would be, by an irony of history, to join forces with the other side, the most hardened traditionalists as well as those of the radical right. Any historical approach of the notion of difference shows that its importance varies, even within one and the same group. Often, blown by the winds of destiny, it shifts, like a pendulum, from a vague background notion to an overglorified affirmation. Its importance is always clearly linked to the meaning that people need to give it at any particular moment. This process can be seen at work in many individuals who at times feel closely allied with their group but at other times may keep their distance and insist on what divides them from it.

When I first began to reflect on these questions, the notion of "difference" did not have a good reputation among those of us involved in anti-colonialist and anti-racist movements. On the contrary, the conservatives and the partisans of colonialism upheld the concept of difference. The arguments advanced by both sides seemed quite clear (and how the wheel of history has turned!). For us, any insistence on difference was suspect, and rightly so; it constituted the very foundation of racist discourse and prepared all its criminal actions. The conservatives, who defend their colonialist social order by basing it on a supposed natural order, accomplished two things at once. They affirmed difference and, by always doing so in their own favor, reduced the colonized to a subhuman level; in treating the colonized as inferior, the colonialists simultaneously constructed themselves as superior. Difference thus signified inequality. Since biological and cultural inequality implied economic and political inequality (i.e., domination), the conservatives gave themselves the right to do as they liked, to do whatever was to their advantage. The same mechanism works against Black people, or against women, to the benefit of Whites, or men. The argument goes that it would be wrong to entrust Black people with the functions of government (and would even be a disservice to them) because it would be contrary to their biological and cultural nature; these responsibilities must be reserved for Whites, who can perform them properly and thus protect everyone's interests. The same holds for women: they must be protected, even from themselves. The authority of men and Whites is thus founded on the delegitimization of women and Blacks. With certain subtle differences, the same mechanism operates with respect to the Jews: "The economic or political success of the Jews would be a disaster for everyone, including the Jews. It is better to prevent it, in the general interest."

In the other camp, namely ours, the commonality and confraternity of all peoples were a matter of principle, based on a very simple metaphysics: only one human nature exists, which is uniform across all time and space. A natural confraternity of people logically implied a *natural* equality: "all men are born free and equal." The small phrase "in rights" had been added by the revolution, but this minor correction, though important, was given scant attention. The main point was that natural equality necessarily implied social equality. Domination, "the exploitation of man by man," was nothing but an abuse, a crime that had to be firmly combated.

While our enemy's position enraged me, there was also something troubling about that of my friends. They affirmed that differences did not exist, from which point everything else followed coherently. If all "men" were "cut from the same cloth," then nothing provided any ground for social inequality except violence and injustice. This generous *Jacobin myopia* derives from the history of the French nation itself, which, in order to constitute itself, fought hard against the particularism or desire for autonomy of certain provinces, at times with terrible excesses.[22] Yet it accepted that leap, even if it were a denial of the real. But what if it were mistaken in its fundamental premises? Suppose difference existed—what would become of the Jacobin position, and in its wake, of *our* entire social philosophy? Would we be obliged to accept the thinking of our adversaries, to resign ourselves to their iniquitous social order, to their colonialism, racism, and masculinism? Such a conclusion was unthinkable to us, though it had a certain logic. If we were to avoid it, there was only one thing to do: submit our own premises to serious review. After all, such things do not depend on opinion but on knowledge. For science, do biological or other differences exist or not, yes or no? The a priori assumption that humans were either the same or different was in either case something that arose from a partisan interest, as a tactic, or from passion. Only the facts could prove one right and the other wrong—or what would be most embarrassing, that differences existed in some cases but not in all.

Let me emphasize this. What I've argued is that differential characteristics can be wholly conceptual, or over-estimated, or simply invented and then imposed on designated groups like a veneer, with no obligation to point out (though not without risk of misunderstanding) what might also be real and objective. This is so for Black people (who have themselves remarked on it), for women, for young people with respect to adults, and again for immigrants, arriving in Europe in greater and greater numbers, who are culturally different and whose real cultural differences sometimes pose certain problems by their proximity. In all these cases, the denial of differential characteristics would obviously not be without serious psychological and sociological significance.

A curious and almost amusing variation on the theme of the systematic erasure of differences is the interpretation of racism found among certain contemporary psychoanalysts.[23] They wish to affirm that racism is built upon a *heterophobia,* a fear of difference, of those who are different, that is, a fear of the unknown. But then they ask, what is this "unknown"? And they respond: it is our own unconscious, which is frightening because it is strange, and which we then project on the other. The advantages of this position are obvious; a denial of objective differences permits one to remain in the realm of analytic theory, just as it enabled the Jacobins to preserve their philosophy of a supposedly homogeneous nation.

Of course, our anxieties do in fact reflect certain inner predispositions toward external danger. A threat or conflict will appear less serious to some than it will to others. Each person responds from his or her own temperament and thus from his or her own unconscious. But to reduce racism or heterophobia to a mere disposition is to lose touch with its specificity, with its many varieties, which in turn depends on its external object and the different forms that can take. Though some disagree with me, I have always maintained that anti-Semitism is a variety of racism, but it is not wholly coincident with other varieties, because each has its own specificity. Racism, in other words, as a pseudo-conceptual construction, may have its source in heterophobia, but it owes much to its particular social and cultural milieu. For instance, there are important differences between the images of the Jews or of women as they appear in literature and religious tradition. If heterophobia lies dormant in everyone, it only takes manifest form in terms of actual events that pose a potential threat; that is, in another who is discerned as no longer phantasmic but rather real, and really different—and sometimes really dangerous. In some cases, shooting first and asking questions afterward, as in Westerns or in the desert, is not always absurd or simply a matter of legend.

Admittedly, in the work of curing, psychoanalysis is mainly interested in what happens in the patient's imagination; what is most important is how the person lives an event, rather than the truth of his or her perception. But it would be detrimental, even for the course of a cure, for the therapist not to know how to differentiate between the real and the imaginary. A friend, caught in a traffic jam, arrived late for his session; he excused himself to his analyst, who responded firmly, "The traffic jam is in your head." The analysis itself is put in question by a refusal to grant equal status to the subject's real world.

In effect, methodology can be abused in such a way as to be disastrous for treatment, for the analytic theory itself, and ultimately for any understanding of a real person. While psychoanalysis may be justified in proposing its own interpretations, they are nevertheless added to others and cannot presuppose that they exhaust all the issues. This recalls Marie Bonaparte's amusing definition of an airplane: it is a phallic symbol that one uses to travel. It took a free spirit, such as this grand dame of psychoanalysis, to dare admonish that the priority given sexual symbolism should not be to the exclusion of the objective or functional dimension of human beings, of things, or of events.

My own thinking soon led me to the unexpected conclusion that both sides, ourselves and our adversaries, had been wrong. Both had fundamentally supposed that *it was bad to be different*. That is, both presupposed, implicitly or explicitly, that a model existed, a good model incarnated in the dominant group.[24] For both, to be different signified to be different from the dominant. In Tunisia, even a liberal and nondenominational schoolteacher, devoted to his "indigenous" Tunisian students, believed himself invested with a mission: to produce little

French people in his own image, the image of France's civilization, its good customs, its refined taste and articulateness. Later, when I went to France (the "Metropole"), I found that the corresponding schoolteacher, the pride of Jacobin democracy, had a similar attitude toward the peasants of his own country, or toward the Bretons or the Alsatians. It was the same old story. For our part, we had to be docile and accede to everything in order to resemble our masters, and we generally did that, even though it meant killing a certain part of our souls.

(And today, in France, we see it happening with respect to the integration of immigrants—the speed with which they are required to learn French culture, as if they, the unfortunate immigrants, more than anyone else, must be the ones to grasp such complex phenomena as cultural differences. Of course, as Descartes advised, it is wise, when living in the midst of another people, not to stand out too much. But it takes time, whose extent cannot be experienced from the outside, for such cultural conversions to occur. To push the process too hard results, on the contrary, in resistance and anguish, because one faces what appears primarily as an abyss on the other side of which assimilation lies. To demand that people renounce their differences too fast is, for them, to demand that they renounce themselves. In addition, it tramples on those feelings of guilt that often accompany those who have emigrated, their vague belief that they have somehow betrayed their own people.)

In sum, like all apparently irresolvable problems, the question of difference had been badly posed—both by the colonialists, who affirmed differences in order to crush the colonized, and by the anti-colonialists, who denied differences in order to protect the colonized. By establishing some distance from the generous but blind republican (anti-colonialist) stance, in order to look directly at what was real, I saw clearly that *differences existed.* What a revelation! How could I have believed for such a long time that they didn't exist! In the street, on the bus, in the markets, the crowd had always been visibly cosmopolitan and diverse! But furthermore, this discovery conceded nothing to racist reasoning, because the diversity was to be found at the interior of each group, including that of any racist, and the boundaries between communities were neither fixed nor clear. We were undeniably different, one from the other.

Later, when I enrolled in the Sorbonne, it made me laugh to hear my companions seriously proclaim that differences between people didn't exist. I let it go, because they had the best intentions in the world. But then, they had only to look at things with their eyes, and not with their minds. In their own country, France, which I traveled through with delight, the population changed from region to region and climate to climate. Everywhere there was this same generosity in all native-born French, this same Jacobin myopia mixed with republican pride—it was an unforeseen outcome of the centralism of the pre-revolutionary aristocratic state *[ancien régime]*. That famous parable of the "forty kings who made France," thanks to "a law, a king, a faith" *[une loi, un roi, une foi]*, reappeared after the revolution in secularized form as the "republic one and indivisible."[25]

During the same period, there were also many seminars and conferences on the reawakening of colonized peoples and the future of colonialism, which began to bring intellectuals together. I attended a number of these meetings. At the first "Congress of Black Intellectuals," I argued that, despite certain notable achievements, the policy of assimilation had been, up to that time, more or less of a failure. Not always, certainly, and not at the hands of the colonized themselves, who had wanted it most of all. But no one else had wanted them. The right refused even to envision such a horror, whose dreaded result would be the mixing of blood and racial impurity *[métissage]*. They feared, of course, that they would thereby lose their privileges. And the left could not imagine working for anything other than what had effectively brought them together themselves. They truly sought a kind of freemasonry of the colonized that would be both socialist and universalist, but not Moslem, fetishist, or Jewish—that is, it would not express the character of each formerly colonized people in its singularity and its own particular differences.

What remained for the colonized (and in general, for all oppressed people, I would later argue) was simply to accept themselves, since no one else would accept them. Where good faith and solicitude had led only to humiliation, only self-vindication remained. There was no other way out. To refuse oneself, to denounce one's defeated ancestors out of shame, to abjure one's language because it was said to be clumsy or one's traditions because they were considered ineffective, was unconscionable. From the moment the oppressed began to speak, they testified to painful and vain acrobatic performances, trying to fulfill the perspective of the dominant, to see themselves through his eyes in order to adopt his perspective, and in the end, they only found themselves living his injurious contempt. To live, one must, in one way or another, affirm oneself.[26] If one cannot affirm oneself through identification with something, one must affirm oneself through difference. To take this one step further: "To be is to be different" (see *Portrait of a Jew*). To affirm one's difference becomes the condition for self-affirmation, the banner for the individual or collective reappropriation of one's self. Where, in the first instance, the dominant affirmed their differences over and against those they oppressed, in the last, the oppressed reclaim their differences against the dominant. I called this second symmetrical movement "the return of the pendulum."

Since then, many experiences have confirmed what has now become the common understanding. But it has not been without pain, occasioned by wrenching and impassioned discussions, by discord and breaks in relations, and by many mistakes. For instance, in several Arab countries, the Jewish citizens, many of whom had contributed to the struggle for national independence, were afterward told to leave. The same happened to the Spanish of the Maghreb. It is rare that the "return of the pendulum" is content merely to correct an unjust situation. Carried away by its own momentum *[élan]*, the pendulum swings far over to the other side, at times perpetrating injustices of its own; thus, there were the expropriations of small colonists and the harassment of minorities who were innocently caught in the situation.[27] Self-affirmation sometimes takes on mythic proportions; to the injurious myths of the past, one counterposes substitute myths that are just as deluded. The least important ancestor becomes a legendary hero, and a folk dance the pinnacle of art. Having struggled for the recognition of differences, I have dissented as well against these new excesses—and do so still. None of them were inscribed in what we had originally sought to reclaim. When, during the first Congress of Black Intellectuals, a participant, recalling Molière, wrote superbly, "I am in rags, perhaps, but these rags are mine," by his intentional use of the word "rags," he refused to hyperbolize his blackness, while at the same time refusing to disown it. As with the slogan "Black is Beautiful" [in English, in the original], one's being a woman, or a Jew, or a Breton can be glorified. Or the Arab Moslem can be proposed as the paragon of civilization. This fierce faith seems to me as debatable as the self-devaluations of the past. No one needs to be ashamed of their past or their heart; to accept oneself is also to accept one's personal and collective history. But is it necessary to pass from self-refusal all the way to hypervaluation? To valorize oneself in excess because one has been devalorized in excess? Does one not risk committing the same errors as the racist partisans of difference? Does one not soon risk affirming oneself against others?

The same holds for other associated notions

that have become popular, such as identity, roots, and so on. If they are difficult to define, they are of doubtful utility as well. All this is explainable as probably necessary after having been downtrodden for so long, but one must watch out for what new delusions one may then confront. It is an irony of history that, whether coming upon or returning to an exaltation of roots and collective identities, the first to preach that exaltation were those of the right. It is no wonder we are witnessing a rebirth of right-wing movements in Europe. At base, it is a movement to recapture the past, and as is often the case, that is an ambiguous project. A common past is generally fictional because it is usually an invention by certain partisan interests, and thus neither common nor a past. One must ask, common to whom? Whose past? The responses to such questions will be full of surprises. Who can really be sure of their supposed ancestors? Some serious research would have to be done . . . if it were possible. And if one really wanted to; I am not sure that many people really wish to disturb their comfortable sense of their own history. In any case, to be is to be different, yes, but to be different is to be other. Therefore, everyone is different and everyone is other. In short, all self-affirmation must be by definition relative. Whatever its importance in one's voyage of recovery, difference cannot be considered an end in and of itself. No one can take the prize in this.

In effect, the real stakes against racism, which must also inform anti-racism, do not concern difference itself but the use of difference as a weapon against its victim, to the advantage of the victimizer.

Therein lies the real depravity of racism. This can all be summed up in three points. Differences can exist or not exist. Differences are not in themselves good or bad. One is not racist or anti-racist in pointing out or in denying differences, but one is racist in using them against someone to one's own advantage.

The Myth and the Alibi

The role of myth-making in the racist undertaking should now be clear (see *A Contre-courants*). If difference exists, it gets interpreted; if it doesn't exist, it gets invented. Elsewhere I have told the story of the psychiatrist who explained to me in all seriousness that the colonized eat badly and walk badly, which would be nothing except that they also breathe badly. Those who dislike manual laborers to the point of repugnance will ultimately find them physically different. In Balzac's descriptions of peasant women, even one of great beauty will at least have large feet to reveal her social origins. His exaggerations are at times so incredible as to be comic. Black men are said to have members of such a size that a woman who had once experienced one could no longer enjoy a White man. All Jews are said to have syphilis, and the women are said to bite off the sex of their lover. What is remarkable is that these disparaging myths, whether funny or not, always devolve to the same basic themes: money, power, and sex, which reveals the preoccupations of the ones who impute the myth. Racism is a mode of behavior, but it is also a discourse, the presentation of a case, both as an accusation and a self-exoneration. The meaning of the argument is hardly in doubt, however; it is always a justification of aggressive hostility.

Thus, the colonialist constructs a portrait of the colonized that is so well adapted to the needs of colonial domination that it presents itself as the predestined order of things. It has been said that Europeans carved out empires for themselves because those whose lives they usurped were simply "colonizable." And how could Europe then refuse its "historical obligation" to fill that "void"? It is even asserted with a straight face that the protectorates were actually established to protect the colonized. The wealth extracted and the burdens imposed were doubtless only the result of thoughtlessness, the excesses of "rogue" elements, as they say these days. Anti-Semites draw mythic figures of Jews that are so well suited to the needs of their passion that one would have to credit it to the very hands of Providence; that is, one must either believe it or pretend to believe it. An example is the role the Jews play in the mythology of Christ, who must fall prey to the Jews in order to redeem humanity. Men expend untold effort painting portraits of women in which women do not recognize themselves, but which the men think are correct! In films of the past, one finds the familiar images of Black people who roll their eyes, stammer and tremble with fear, unable to live without the protective "custody" of menial labor after having emerged from enslavement. All these portraits are convenient, betraying an atmosphere of familiarity that fulfills the needs and fantasies of the oppressors.

This utility finds itself embarrassed neither by incoherence nor by immoderation. No obstacle will prevent a racist from being derogatory. The Jew, for instance, is seen as *simultaneously* avaricious and wasteful, a woman is seen to be both artless and deceitful. Even the most admirable qualities are transformed into defects. The Jews have an intelligence that has been sharpened by hardship; yes, but then, they are too intelligent, which only makes them more dangerous. Is the Jew accommodating and inclined toward conciliation? No, he is obsequious; it is a ruse. Are Black people endowed with a sense of rhythm? It is the proof of their unfitness for more noble pursuits. The softness of women is only a result of their natural passivity, their lack of combativity. Nothing of the prey of these attacks is safe from this systematic machinery of dark defamation. The Jew presents, simultaneously, a biological, economic, psychological, cultural, and metaphysical figure . . . and *every* aspect is negative. It is not that Jews, the colonized, or women might not have different adequacies or inadequacies. I have already discussed the importance of not allowing oneself to deny all the differences. But in racist discourse, it is the oppressed who have nothing but faults, while the dominant have all the virtues! Why is every way in which the dominated differ seen as bad, a priori? Why must the dominant systematically denounce the other's mode of being, their customs (even the most banal), their expressions of joy as well as their evidence of pain, their ways of cooking and their ways of teaching ("How could they eat that!" or "Here the children are the most poorly raised in the world"). It is true even where one claims to make exceptions, like those anti-Semites who have a Jewish "friend," or in the corrosive irony against *all* women: "They're all no good, except my mother, who is a saint." It is said as a joke, of course, but one that is not entirely innocent.

Is it not that such vehement derogation, even in its incoherence, in one way or another, might be useful to the one who spews the venom? After all, the comparisons are *always* in his favor. Who does not see that the racist reconstructs his prey in accordance with his own needs? The mythic reconstruction of the other serves him as mediation, a specific alibi for the oppression he seeks to impose or that is already imposed: men over women, Whites over Blacks, the colonizer over the colonized. This only highlights the particular effectiveness of the biological argument; it provides the best assurance. The Black is irremediably black, the woman is irremediably a woman. Thus, we encounter the undying efforts to biologically characterize the Jew and the colonized, even though biology is irrelevant. *Biology is a metaphor for the destiny imposed on the other.*

Racism and Oppression

Whatever its little detours may be, ultimately, *the goal of racism is dominance.* This is the last point I will elicit from its relation to colonialism. It is a point of correlation, however, that provides an essential insight into the structure of racism. As in billiards, where one aims at one ball in order to hit another, though racism levies its accusatory derogations under many different pretexts, it does so always in order to reject, to injure, and to oppress. In looking first at the colonial relation, I was led to elucidate and then systematize that same relation in other forms of racism, those enmeshed in other, yet similar, conditions of oppression. Of course, the case of the Jews, with which I preoccupied myself next, was one I knew from the inside, without having to reflect on it. But the elaboration of my general reflections in *The Colonizer and the Colonized* also came naturally. Then, by passing from the colonial situation to other forms of oppression, I was able to extend the formula given above: *racism illustrates and symbolizes oppression.*

That said, if we now reexamine the importance of myth in the racist discourse, we can see its limits. It is necessary, but it is relative; it is crucial, but it is not the whole of racism. *Racism is an opinion, but it is an opinion that declares an intention and signals a mode of conduct.*

One opinion does not suffice to make a racist, assuming he could stop there. Racism is both the ideology and the active manifestation of domination. Each time one explores a relation of oppression, one discovers within it a racism, like a ghost or a shadow, as its inevitable extension. An aspect of all forms of dominance, it is a laborious and self-concerned form of bad faith. If I dominate you, it is *because* you are an inferior being; the responsibility is yours, and the differences that exist between us prove it. Whites can exploit *[asservir]* Blacks because Blacks are not White—that is, they are afflicted with the insufficiency of being Black, and thus deprived of the virtue of being White. Men have the right to use women because women are different and because femininity is a deficiency. Whatever the seductions of those deficiencies, a certain distorted conduct is authorized: one can be a "ladies' man" and still have contempt for women; one can be infatuated with Black women or Jewish women, or Arab boys, without ceasing to despise the world each comes from.

Thus, the general effect of the dominance-subjection relation is to destroy both parties, each by the other, and each in a specific manner. Though the corrosive suffering of the victim is wholly incommensurate with and overshadows the psychic deformation of the victimizer, one nevertheless does not transform oneself into an executioner without great cost. There is a double erosion of personhood in all racism, because its only purpose is to torment other people through an attempt to reduce them to nothing, and to harass people to the point of destroying them. I do not mean this symbolically, or as a moment of the racist's imagination, but as a concrete process of constant humiliation, of gratuitous constraint imposed on the other's life; at its worst, the other finally engages in forms of self-destruction. That is, the *interiorization* of racist denigration is not the least criminal aspect of it; it is the ingestion of a poison that eats away from the inside, and whose end is the victim's wholehearted adoption of the imposed image. How is one to defend oneself if one is driven into agreement with one's persecutor? Before the French Revolution, a person named Moreau de Saint-Mery developed a classification of the people of the Antilles that included "negroes," "mulattoes," "quadroons," *métis, mamelouques, sang-mêlés, marabouts, griffés,* and *sacatros,*[28] along with various other designations. When I went to the Antilles myself, I was shocked to find that Saint-Mery's schema was not only still in effect, but enriched! The people of the Antilles had adopted and preserved this infernal scale of diminished dignity, measured by a person's distance from the "White Father" (their own expression), with all the implicit social and psychological damage one might imagine. The scars of past oppression are not easily healed. It reminded me of a Tunisian concierge who became very angry at me one day but could only express it through a reflection on herself: "You are nothing but a Tunisian, like us!"

Yet one's racism is not a road to paradise, either. Because it is bad faith, it demands constant defense, argument, and hostility. It is a bottomless pit, an endless debate in which no one is ever completely convinced—neither those victimized, despite their harassment and torment, nor those who think in racist terms and who sense their lack of being, their obsessive need for an endless campaign that never brings them peace of mind. During my trip to the Antilles, I spent time with many *Békés* (French people born on the islands), and they never stopped talking about "all that."

Let it be said in passing (I will return to this later) that the necessity for endless defensiveness and self-explanation is not a totally bad sign. At the risk of sounding confused, I would say that, in a manner of speaking, the racist deserves some credit. A hardened criminal does not talk, he kills. But behind racism's evil aspect, there is something that could be called *the ethical paradox of the racist stance,* and it offers a glimmer of hope. Animals devour their prey without due process when they are hungry. More vigorous plants tend to crowd out the weaker. Humans, like all living things, seize, crush, or kill, both their own kind and others. But they find it necessary to talk about it as well, to explain and to justify themselves to others, to obtain approbation. Do I dominate? Do I have privileges? Certainly, but it is because I have rights! On this land, my father, after all . . . my ancestors . . . and so on. It is a pitiful legitimacy, of course, fallacious, fictional, and out of joint. But it is proclaimed, insisted on, and even theorized. There are philosophies and moralities founded on race, psychology, sex, culture, and metaphysics. One does for oneself what one can for the sake of a slightly easier conscience. How much of the behavior of "grand" families or of "national" politics is nothing more than rapaciousness at the level of the group? Yet still, the necessity to rationalize it as preserving a sacred familial patrimony or the "national interest" remains inescapable. In one way or another, the need to justify one's gains is ineluctable.

The Advantage

There is always some benefit or advantage to be gained. That is the very thing that commands attention: *the racist undertaking is never disinterested,* even if what it seeks to gain is not immediately evident.

What would the advantage be? Of what could it consist? On the surface, it could be anything: psychological, economic, political, cultural . . . whatever one seeks, more or less consciously, to the detriment of the other. At the risk of redundancy, we can define the benefits of racism as *all that produces an advantage or privilege through the devaluation of the other.*

An objection that Marxism might raise should perhaps be addressed. For most Marxists, the diversity of racism's social advantages is a deception, in the strong sense of the term. "Man" is, essentially, an economic animal, driven principally by economic needs. The rest is diversion, ruse, and ideology. In these terms, racism is fundamentally an economic weapon. Racist discourse becomes an alibi disguising an interminable appropriation of natural resources and, more to the point, the "exploitation of man by man." According to the familiar formula, "economics is the ultimate motor of history."

I am in partial agreement with the Marxists here. They are right to suspect that racism seeks another end, behind all its disparagements and attacks. I am quite convinced that there are usually two levels to a discourse—an explicit content and a hidden meaning. Often, the hidden meaning is much more important and more revelatory than the literal. For racism, the real meaning must be mystified in order not to reveal its basic injustice. Its primary need is to fool its prey, to forestall their reactions, which would be counteractive. But also, oppression needs disguises for itself as well; it is not always possible to assent to privilege with an easy conscience. At times, an iron-fisted regime becomes necessary, which is not particularly pleasant to live in and, moreover, is costly. A good disguise or an adroit defense is worth the effort, at least as an economy of means. One virtue of the ideology of domination is that it is pragmatic—which contributes to its stability and power.

The Marxists are not wrong, either, in suspecting contemporary racism of economic motivation. Frequently, that is the case, though it may not always be evident. Examples are not hard to find in history, sociology, or even literature. The small anti-Semitic businessman enmeshed in his problems, or a victim of his own greed, will hope to gain immediate benefit from the destruction of his Jewish competitors. It is not an accident that economic recession always seems to call up the lurking monster of anti-Semitism.

My agreement with the Marxists ends there. I think they are wrong to think that privilege always reduces itself to economic advantage—even as "ultimate determinant," according to their customary expression. Which is, of course, an ambiguous formula; if one rejects consideration of intermediary forms, it becomes false, while if one admits the importance of these forms, then the formula has only theoretical interest. A similar argument would apply to explanations based on the Oedipus complex, for instance. I am well aware that it is no longer possible to lump all Marxists together. Having aged, the doctrine has become diversified, as with old religions, and the faithful wisely counsel tolerance toward dissident sects and heretics. Marxists, however, even those who no longer support the necessity of one exclusive interpretation, still accept the primacy of economics "in the final analysis" (as they say). Yet it suggests, more or less directly, an economic determinism. Human reality is more complex; one could not know for certain what unique factor governs all the rest, nor could one know even if such a thing exists. Human needs are multiple, even if they are not endlessly multiplied. Priorities are variable and fluid. The need for security, or the need for love, is often as important as the need for nourishment. In short, one might adopt a racist stance for many different reasons, and not simply for calculable economic return—even though, for all, the mechanism whereby those gains are achieved may be the same.

The Scapegoat

The phenomenon of the scapegoat illustrates this point. The Ancients had an extraordinary intuition. To exorcise misfortune, they sacrificed an expiatory animal to the gods; by loading the poor beast with all the sins of the community, they thus unburdened it of its collective guilt. The notion of a tragic hero works in a similar way, and it is no accident that this was so successful as theater. Accused of being the source of whatever calamities have struck, the hero must perish in order to bring them to an end. In some cases, he is not responsible, being instead a pawn of fatal destinies (like Oedipus) or of occult divine machinations. Whatever the case, the collective conscience does not recoil from choosing an innocent person to pay for the crimes and comforts of others. The myth of Jesus Christ is of this genre: a man of good repute and purity of being who, as a saint and son of a virgin, is designated to redeem the sufferings and sins of humanity. Agamemnon sacrificed his daughter as virginal martyr in order to appease the wrath of the gods, as if her purity, like clean linen, was needed to wipe away the stains of former corruption. It is as if the purity of the victim becomes the coin with which to pay the costs charged by destiny or divinity.[29] Naturally, such an interpretation does not exhaust these myths. But what it signifies is that to load one's mistakes and misfortunes upon another makes an adverse situation more tolerable, whether the sacrificial victim is a competitor or a neighbor, a member of a minority or of another nation, an institution or nature itself. To attribute our private or public failures, our sports or professional defeats, to the treachery of an adversary excuses our own deficiencies. In the film *The Little Soldier,* Charlie Chaplin's hero shoots at a stone, which he holds responsible for his misfortunes. Isn't this what the bigot does? Or as a humorist once said, "Why the Jews, and not bicyclists?" To which the anti-Semite would reply: "Because the Jews fill the bill."

The derogatory stance, the act of denigrating another, permits people to close ranks with each other; the identification of an external threat, whether real or imagined, restores fraternity. Our modern leaders have only revived a very old recipe; one has only to designate a responsible party, however innocent she or he may be, to vindicate the rest. Name the misfortune, give it a face, and thereby create the illusion of having mastered it! The effect is to assuage the collective self as much as the individual self.

For these purposes, the marginalized are "well placed," as they say in horse racing. Foreigners are less protected by the law; minorities, or those who are different, are already suspect. They make excellent hooks on which to hang collective anxiety. It is not an accident that the inquisitions of Europe killed so many female witches and so few male ones. Women are different and less adept at defending themselves. General fear and resentment are more easily incorporated in them. In more recent times, Black people in the United States have been burned by lynch mobs, as women were burned during the Inquisition. The genocidal[30] campaign against the Jews, in which fully a third of the world's Jews were exterminated, was the latest avatar of this ongoing butchery. To exteriorize evil by incarnating it in another separates it from society and renders it less threatening. It can be manipulated, managed, destroyed by fire. The common denominator must be understood: fire purifies all, including ourselves . . . but only by burning the other. That is where it is most economical.

These are extreme cases, in which the inner meanings are more clearly seen, but the same meanings can then be discovered in other places and other events. At the individual level, one destroys in the other what one would like to destroy in oneself, by imputing to that other one's own faults. Indeed, it is the vehemence of the apologies, the excessive protestations about our own virginal innocence against the baseness of the other, that betrays as much as it affirms. The protestations are too shrill. The outcome of the trial is never in question; the victim is convicted in advance, with the public in solidarity with the prosecution. And the executioners, whether they work with hot coals or words, whether they roast their enemies or only designate them as such, always proclaim for themselves a great love for the collective soul. Through them, we are no longer the guilty, because the other is. Of course, we are never wholly convinced, since we must continue to argue and debate. But even these efforts, though a furtive avowal of our deficiencies, become a part of our self-purification. Like ritual baths, they are more effective when all take them together. We evoke our faults in common; we account for and cleanse ourselves collectively. Henceforth, we are pure, because we all participate in the same purity. What transcends and envelops us we have drawn out of ourselves, and we now find the evil outside, beyond us. Thus, we give ourselves mutual self-absolution.

One could go on about the necessity for purity. Having already found biological purity to be inconceivable, we have dispensed with its pretenses. *Psychological purity is no more intelligible* (see *A Contre-courants*). But why is there such an obsessive preoccupation with it? The answer is easy: since purity cannot be documented, it can only appear as a promise, made at the behest of a nostalgia or a hope. The racist mind aspires to the image of a perfect nation, though one it is nevertheless unable to really describe. One finds it difficult to say if the ideal is a return to a former state or the establishment of a new order, a lost paradise, or a messianic golden age. The Italian fascists combined the two: ancient Rome and the avant-garde of European modernity. The Pan-German movement conjured up a past splendor as legitimation for imposing its rule on the world. In general, a future seen as a projection of the past is amalgamated with a past reconstructed as a function of the future. It is both a regret for not living in that past state of grace and a desire to recapture it. And against all intruders, all those strangers who threaten to tarnish or obstruct the enactment of promised communion, however illusory it might be, there is recourse to a familiar violence. In that moment, one comes face to face with the scapegoat.

The trauma and drama of this process have seduced philosophers and inspired poets. Even psychoanalytic interpretations suggest themselves: "Ah, how good it was to be all *together,* myself between Papa and Mama, in the warmth of the home, sheltered from the cold external world!" "Ah, how good it was *before* that new baby arrived, that shitting, pissing stranger who has polluted everything, disturbed the family harmony, absorbed all the milk, monopolized all parental love and the attentions of visitors." But while the poets dream, and philosophers and psychologists interpret, the racist acts. Since a return to the carefree world of infancy is impossible, he says, let us make a future in its image; let us constitute our homogeneity in solidarity *against* all who disturb or defile it; let us rid ourselves of the intruders, the immigrants, the invaders, the polluters, by means of their destruction if necessary. And I wonder if the desecraters of Jewish tombs, the ragged slanderers and occasional assassins of poor immigrant workers, do not get some real sensual pleasure from committing their crimes, though they have probably convinced themselves that they act for the public good. Indeed, many participants in white lynch mobs have acknowledged a kind of deranged ecstasy in defending the mythic integrity of the white race. This miserable plague, this scandal, which I have already shown is delusory, must be brought to an end if a life-affirming social order is to be established. There are children who would kill that unacceptable little brother if they could, and sometimes they can. The obsession with purity arises from a fear of pollution and a vow to obviate it.

Racism and Anti-Semitism

The condition of the Jews, seen through my experience with colonialism, convinced me that racism required the intimate daily participation of individuals who had a need for some kind of victim. This also suggested to me the truly *extensive character of the structure of racism.* Anti-Semitism is a particularly clear example because it represents the exclusion of a group that is in closest possible proximity.

The claim has been made that anti-Semitism is totally different from racism. I would disagree. Although it does not resemble any other form of social exclusion, it is not any less a variety of racism for all that. *It is a racism specific to its object.* That is, anti-Semitism is racism directed against Jews. As such, it has a particular character that it acquires from its particular victims and from the original relation between them and those who attack them. The Jew–anti-Semite binary encompasses a figure of victimization that is unlike any other: the Jews, as a very ancient minority, are both familiar and alien; their culture is both strange and recognizable, with social structures that reveal affinity yet are autonomous. Anti-Semitism avails itself of an effective and well-worn mythology in which the long history of disparagement and oppression, the place the Jews have been given in the economic system, their role in cultural tradition, and their assurance of election, all come together. The relationship of the Jews to their persecutors, whether Christian or Moslem, is more reminiscent of warring brothers than of perfect strangers. Despite the animosity, which at times is murderous, the Christians recognize their kinship with the Jews. "Spiritually, we are Semites," Pope Paul VI once recalled. The Moslems as well insist on community with the Jews as "peoples of the book." Nevertheless, all things considered, while anti-Semitism may have its own peculiarity, it nevertheless belongs in the category of racist relations. Like them, it is an act of stigmatizing the other for one's own consolation, through the deployment of respective differences. That is, "*their* differences are ugly and wrong, while *ours* are good and beautiful, and it is by the grace of this comparison that we have overcome them."

What grows from this, unexpectedly, is the necessity to exacerbate the differences—an effect that is encountered everywhere—to fortify ours and emphasize theirs. Mixed marriage, for example, must be vigorously condemned. Promiscuity must be prevented at all costs as a catastrophe for the species. Everyone should preserve their own character, their identity, as they say these days. The Bible itself does not sanction mixed marriages, which it associates with paganism! (See, in particular, the Book of Ezra.) Of course, such marriages have been an ever-present tendency; hence, the strictness of Jewish law, which will produce, despite itself, a vast progeny. Barrès cultivated his self . . . but also those of others; Lyautey wanted to "respect" the Moroccan Islamic personality, and he was sincere even if this respect resembled a suffocating embrace. The most unrepentant masculinists swear by "the eternal feminine." The Christians have never desired the complete disappearance of the Jews; what they required was that the Jews, through their humiliation, eternally testify to the glory of Christianity's difference. That the Arabs must remain Arabs and the Jews remain Jews becomes an unforeseen and ironic consequence of ecumenism. I once asked François Mauriac, who campaigned under this banner, why he tried so hard to persuade Moslems to remain Moslems. He answered me honestly: "So that the Christians remain Christians."

Contradictions? How could one desire the annihilation of someone and at the same time preserve them in their own body? The racist mind, we repeat, has contradictions to spare. But it is there that racist behavior really reveals its inner coherence; as with all domination, the racist needs to control his prey to the point of impoverishment, almost to the point of death, just barely preserving the other's life and energy . . . in order to continue to use it. The structure of this operation with respect to the colonized is familiar. The boundary between colonization and premeditated murder is created and sustained by the needs of the colonizer. Without that, it reduces to death and genocide. For example, the first European settlers in the Americas decimated the Indians because they did not have a way of using them, of making them work. Later, to meet the needs of plantation labor, they resorted to importing Black (African) laborers, then South Americans, and finally people from India.

This is why, to understand any given form of racism, one must inquire into what benefit a particular racist group gains over the particular group they have picked as a target, as their prey. That is, beyond general mechanisms, what does the anti-Semite seek in anti-Semitism, the masculinist man through masculinism, the colonialist through colonization? And what is each of them looking for at any particular historical moment?

THE LESSONS OF HISTORY

The response to these questions resolves another difficulty: how to reconcile the longevity and tenacity of racism with the belatedness of its "theories."[31]

The problem is important because the relative modernity of racist "thought" has been a source of misunderstanding. Some people wish to see racism as only a passing phenomenon, since it has not always existed. They try to contend, though in vain, that coherent racist arguments are not to be found deep in the past. In their view, the first theoretician of consequence would be Gobineau, whose *Essay on the Inequality of Human Races*[32] appeared in 1854. But they are not correct. Biological differences have been used for a long time. Early legitimation of the African slave trade proposed to view the slaves as quasi-animal in nature. In addition, the existence of counter-theoretic refutations points to precisely such theoretic ambitions, to which they oppose themselves; Montesquieu, for instance, in order to deride it, reviews the reasoning of the slave traders. Before 1492, the date of the expulsion of the Jews from Spain, the myth of blood and bloodline already obsessed the Spanish, or at least their ruling classes. Earlier still, Tacitus (56–120 A.D.) stigmatized the people of Judea (the Jews of that period) for their physical and moral defects. Appian of Alexandria (second century A.D.), among others, proclaimed the biological impurity of the Jews to be the cause of leprosy. Evidently, nothing is new under the sun.

It is true, however, that racism as a systematic and rationalized hostility based on biological differences is relatively recent. On the other hand, there has always existed a suspicion of strangers and of those who are different. In the past, biology commanded less attention, and it had a narrower scope; it is new as a science. But the documents are legion, both sacred and profane, that speak of the dread that outsiders inspire and the hostility aroused by fear. Actually, the stranger is the origin of very ambiguous feelings, because one does not know exactly who one is dealing with. The outsider provokes a malaise that involves both distrust and respect. An unknown voyager who asks for a drink of water or a night's lodging could be a sinister messenger or the envoy of God, like the angel who foretold the birth of Isaac to the aged Sarah. The stranger could be the incarnation of the devil or a deity in disguise, like the avatars of pagan gods. In either case, whether a joyous event or the onset of the plague, a disastrous upheaval or a windfall for one and all, it is best to be vigilant. The problem is that the passage from suspicion to self-defense, and from self-defense to aggression, is easily done.

Anti-Semitism is again a good example of this ambivalence toward difference. The history of anti-Semitism is today well known. In the ancient world, it most often took the form of a phobia, an irrational aversion, usually of a cultural rather than a religious nature. Judean beliefs and customs, because relatively unknown, were generally fantasized, and thus became a source of anxiety. Bernard Lazare insists that what he calls the obstinacy of the Jews constituted the source of ancient anti-Semitism.[33] It is possible, but it is also undeniable that every minority can be accused of a certain exceptionalism . . . by a majority that requires its assimilation, that is, its disappearance to the majority's benefit. "Judeophobia" can be understood as a particular form of xenophobia, which was itself common throughout the Hellenic world and Egypt against any people who came from elsewhere. In effect, while one can possibly date the appearance of racism in the strict sense, one cannot do so for xenophobia.

It is this notion, the operation of xenophobia, that I find lacking in the books of Jules Isaac, which are otherwise so rich and useful, so meticulous and convincing in their investigations. Isaac argues that a hostility *specifically* against the Jews emerges only around the first century, with the appearance of Christianity. For him, it was a question of religious competition. Of course, biology was not relevant, especially since the first Christians were themselves Jews. Biological differences do not become an issue until later, in Spain. At that moment a racist tradition in its modern sense really begins. After that, a "theoretic" elaboration is constructed by various German and French "thinkers," along with its murderous translation into the many pogroms of Europe and Russia, and its pinnacle in the total genocide almost realized by the Nazis and their henchmen.

But in any case, whether it is "Judeophobia" or "anti-Semitism," whether it is biological or not, History confirms it as being racist. For instance, as Jules Isaac points out, Christian anti-Semitism (again, poorly named, since the first Christians were Jews) systematically demonized the Jews. But why such a system? Why put in place an actual machinery of denigration? Was it to be the herald of so much eventual butchery? To answer this question, we have but to turn to authors of the time, such as John Chrysostome (347–407 A.D.) or Saint Augustine (354–430 A.D.). The denigration of the Jews was, for them, *necessary for the exaltation of the Christians.*

The new but still fragile Christianity, in order to thrive, had to separate itself cleanly from its initial roots. It had to forge its own origin, in order not to be confused with the other; that is, to fortify itself of necessity against that other. This was the task of the first Christian writers. Doctrinal distinctions do not lie at the origin of Christian anti-Semitism but rather political and demographic necessity, though it later led to a search for and deployment of doctrinal differences. In other words, the goal of Christian anti-Semitism was, for newly born Christianity, not a question of biology or economics, but of collective self-affirmation.

The genesis of Arab anti-Semitism (also poorly named, because of their great ethnic and linguistic proximity) differs little from this pattern. At first, the prophet Mohammed showed no real hostility to the Jews of Medina,[34] hoping to win them to his cause. He recognized in them the most ancient "people of the Book." And indeed, to have won them over would have proved the preeminence of his message. But the seduction did not work; those old veterans of messianism, jaded by their own long line of messiahs, did not take this new candidate seriously. So he changed his strategy. Unable to affirm himself through the Jews, he affirmed himself against them. Chosen to bear witness to his grandeur, they were to become the proof of it through their own debasement. The war he made on them, in the name of Islam, was first a war of arms, followed later by a war of words. Luther would follow more or less the same pattern—as would the later inheritors of the

Arab prophet, for whom it became quite prosaic. Because they were vanquished, the Jews were to be progressively downtrodden by ever-conquering Arabs during the long unfolding of Islamic expansionism. They were forced to pay an economic tribute; for what did one fight a war if not to profit from it? As for a cause to justify this racket, doctrine came to the rescue: this is how one must treat enemies of the true faith, even if they are not total strangers but cousins by blood and by culture. From then on, economic profit is simply added to spiritual profit. And the spiritual benefit will never disappear; the latter-day texts will forever attest to it. The Jew is contemptible because he is defeated, weak, and disarmed, but also because he is living testimony to bad faith and blindness—he knows the Truth better than anyone but does not want to recognize it. Hence the historic tribulation; hence, conversely, the just glory of the conqueror. It is the same curious mixture of aggressivity and satisfaction with respect to the Jews that is found among the Christians. In short, the Arabs do not oppress the Jews because they are anti-Jewish; they are anti-Jewish because they oppress the Jews.[35]

Later, when the Spanish spoke of a purity of blood (their own, naturally), they were implicitly suggesting that that of others, Jews and Moors, was impure. But strictly speaking, that makes no sense, except perhaps as a kind of vague fear of the Marranos,[36] who were generally fairly secretive about themselves. One can also view it as a metaphor, however, comparable to the sentiment expressed in the French national anthem. In the *Marseillaise,* "the impure blood that waters our fields" was that of the enemy, which can be sung without remorse. Indeed, one kills two birds with one stone: one also fertilizes the fields. Similarly, the idea of the purity of Spanish blood was, in a manner of speaking, a convenient ploy *[un outil commode]*. It radically separated the Christian nobles from the Jews, even the converted ones (conversion is not sufficiently purifying for the blood); thus, it set the nobility's power apart and out of reach. In addition, against the political influence of converted Jews and Moors, it functioned to consolidate the unity of the Spanish nation, which had just emerged from a long corrosive period of instability. But there is also a sexual dimension to collective obsession with "purity of blood." During successive occupations, Spain had been subjected to what one might discreetly call fraternization but which was really sororization, since the issue was relations between the Spanish women and the invaders. Rarely did the opposite occur; the Spanish men were deemed a source of possible betrayal, so their union with the foreign woman was tolerated only under highly regulated circumstances. In the end, the proclamation of an indelible purity of Spanish "blood" became a way to deny the damage, the unspeakable shame of having had so many women defiled. It was another kind of gain.

One final example, the closest to us: Nazism. That cataclysm, whose ruins are still being cleared away, as much in our souls as in our cities, has fascinated the world with its horror. That is, I suppose, because it went to the limit: a maximum of cynicism and a minimum of ethics. All racism attempts some form of self-rationalization. On that score, the Nazis unreservedly made the stakes of their conquest very plain; it was of no importance to them who or what would be sacrificed for the construction of a greater Germany. In this, the concept of gain itself was purified. It also sheds a pale light on the almost incomprehensible monstrosity of Nazi procedures. If, in comparison to the goal pursued, a human being no longer has any value, she or he merely becomes a utilitarian object. Soap can be made from human fat, lamp shades from human skin, and cloth from human hair. Yet even this utmost horror remained flexible. For the Nazis, a "theory" of the Jews as an absolute disease of the social body was to be pronounced, but even that was not unalterable when other needs arose. They used the labor of Jews when they needed laborers and the mythic image of the Jew when they needed material for their propaganda. Utility was always in command; it was just not always the same utility.

In this regard, the Jews were particularly convenient. All the negative stereotypes were already in place; they had simply to be deployed to redirect German aggressiveness, as any conquered people is used. Without territorial refuge, the Jews could offer no resistance, nor did they have recourse to any real protection. Aggression could be heaped on them with impunity, to the point of mass murder—which is what happened. But the Nazis did the same thing to the Gypsies, the homosexuals, to whomever they considered subhuman. It is interesting to note that in each of these cases, the target was an undefended minority. In *Mein Kampf,* Hitler gave notice of the necessity to rid Europe of Black people. The French, whom he accused of "Negrifying" themselves and of having brought their corrupt blood to the banks of the Rhine, would have to be subjected to serious cleansing. What would have happened if the Nazis had won the war?

Thus, the lessons of history are clear. Racism does not limit itself to biology or economics or psychology or metaphysics; *it attacks along many fronts and in many forms,* deploying whatever is at hand, and even what is not, inventing when the need arises. To function, it needs a focal point, a central factor, but it doesn't care what that might be—the color of one's skin, facial features, the form of the fingers, one's character, or one's cultural tradition. . . . If none of this works, it will propose a mythical trait, perhaps concerning a particular quality of the blood or an ancestral curse. One has simply to look to find what will bolster the most fantastic story: a rumor, perhaps, or some obscure commentary on a traditional text. Even the clashes between the Jews and their own God were used against them—did not this signify they had been designated by God for universal persecution? I remember, as a child, hearing of the origins of Black servitude in the story of Noah's three sons, retold in utmost seriousness. Shem begat the Semites, who received the Law; Japheth begat the people of the North, who were bequeathed technical knowledge; and Ham begat the Hamites, who are the Black people, and who . . . got nothing. And there you have the reason your daughter is taciturn, or why the Europeans can, with the blessings of Providence, dominate the Africans. It was the first example of explaining the colonization of a people by their "colonizability." The reality of the situation is wholly beside the point; what is essential is that racism rests upon and functions as a kind of seesaw: *the persecutor rises by debasing and inferiorizing his victim.*

The Testimony of the Victims . . .

In the course of time, opportunities have arisen to illustrate or substantiate some of these ideas, mostly by fortuitous means. During the first stages of my research, I had relied primarily on my own experience, proceeding by intuition and logic. But I had no way of corroborating my analyses; I was confined to description *[montrer],* where what I needed was demonstration *[démontrer].* Fate provided the latter in two forms: correspondence from the readers of my works, and a semi-sociological inquiry initiated by an anti-racist movement, the MRAP.[37]

Following the publication of my books on the colonial relation, I received many letters describing how the patterns and structures I had brought to light were relevant in other areas. Some readers in Quebec, for example, claimed that life with the English Canadians was of a colonial modality. They invited me to Quebec to see for myself. When I finally visited them sometime later, I found I had both to confirm their views and to attentuate them somewhat. First, the semi-colonial relations that tied them to Anglophone Canada were subtly transformed by the absence and omnipresence of a third partner in their situation: the United States. Second, to the extent that Quebec was in a colonial situation, its relative richness made it economically enviable; it was unusual in that respect. Finally, it had an extraordinary rapport with France, the country of origin of the families of Quebec. France had become a mythic benchmark and a point of historical reference, even a source of nostalgia, though the two countries had developed in quite disparate directions. Thus, though Quebec had a certain resemblance to a traditional colony, specific aspects had to be taken into account. On the other hand, it was clear that among the English Canadians, one encountered many aspects of the colonialist mind. They had nothing but a badly concealed disdain for the customs, culture, or language of the Quebecois, which they used to their benefit. It was clearly within the pattern of racism, at least in its evident ostracism. The Francophone people truly suffered from this, from which the Anglophones gained certain advantages that were not simply economic. I conveyed this view in several articles, including an interview, "Are the French Canadians Colonized?" (in *Dominated Man*), which caused some commotion and has since been reprinted often in Quebec.

Around the same time, newly developing feminist movements were adopting slogans such as "Women are the colonized of men" and "The woman is the proletarian of the man," which, though founded on reality, did not seem to me to be wholly adequate.

The economic dimension, though of central importance, is not the essential factor in the oppression of women. Any woman alone on the street has cause to fear, whatever her social status. A transformation of economic conditions will probably not suffice to change those circumstances. (Indeed, there is an inverse example: it is arguable that the birth control pill has done more for women than all the union struggles and the volumes of rhetoric combined.[38]) The colonial structure also does not exhaustively describe the relation between men and women because of the specific complexities of that relation, namely, its foundation on emotional attraction and reciprocal dependence, together with the existence of common parental responsibility. The colonizer and the colonized do not fall in love with each other, nor do they relate, in and of itself, erotically. However, beyond such notable or evident differences, one encounters the common characteristics of a relation of oppression: a systematic devaluation of women from which men draw many advantages—all men, from all women. I tried to explicate all this in my writing. I felt quite honored when a young feminist movement contacted me; it called itself MFA, or Masculine–Feminine–Future *[Masculin–Feminin–Avenir],* and later became the MLF, or movement for the liberation of women. I dedicated to this group a text about Simone de Beauvoir, titled "In Defense of a Tyrant," the tyrant being myself, the author, representing all men.

But it was the encounter and the subsequent friendships with Black Americans that were the most enlightening for me. In questions such as these, one most often hears only the oppressor's side—which is not surprising, since he generally has control of the media. He accuses, he denigrates, he imposes his law, he explains himself in order to legitimate his persecutions. The one subjected to all this can usually only groan, to which a deaf ear is most often turned. Should the oppressed wish to make their case heard, they will have a problem. The voice of the oppressed is not given a ready hearing—that is, when it is not systematically silenced. Often, feeling their impotence, or worse, having interiorized their defeat, the oppressed resign themselves to saying nothing.[39] On this score, the voice of Black Americans surprised me with its vigor, its vitality, and, in a way, with its audacity. For example, unlike most oppressed peoples, Black Americans speak openly of their biology. It is seldom that those in a minority, the colonized, the Jews, or other oppressed groups will be the ones to raise the question of biological differences.[40] The dominant deploy those ideas against those they dominate, as defamatory discourses, and the latter are simply left to react to it as best they can. The Jews actually find their biological portrait derisive—and even a sign of the intellectual feebleness and perversity of their persecutors. But Black Americans take their physical description seriously and react to it in many ways. In this regard, their approach is similar to that of women. I had noted in an early article that Black people seemed to spend a fair amount of time trying to lighten their complexion or straighten their hair. A lot has changed since then. Again, the return of the pendulum: now they accentuate their particularities and wear their hair in the manner of Black Africans. After having suffered many insults to the body, they exalt it. Indeed, one now sees Whites adopting similar styles in solidarity. Many young people try to identify to the extent of making themselves look African (or at least so they imagine) with huge masses of curly hair for the men, and many fine braids, adorned with beads, for the women.

I have discussed (above, and elsewhere) the idea of the "return of the pendulum" and the use of countermyths; I don't need to do so again. While I understand what its excesses are about, I refuse to encourage them. I feel strongly that the oppressed do themselves a disservice to march in lockstep with phantasms, whatever they may be. After all, it is no more legitimate to proclaim that God is Black than to proclaim that he is White. It is no more marvelous to have black skin and a flat nose than to have white skin and a pointed nose. It is no more glorious to have a vagina than a penis, or the inverse. It is not a virtue to be Black, or Jewish, or female, just as it is not a virtue to be White or Male.

But that said, the countermyth, whether biological or not, must be understood as a response, like that of the shepherdess in the black sheep story. It is both inevitable and necessary (though one hopes not for too long a time) that Black people extol their particular biological being. They could not indefinitely refuse the fight that had been thrust on them. A Black friend once said to me, with sadness, "A Jew is not obliged to declare himself a Jew, but how can I pass unseen?" Where White people had long declared large lips to be an anomaly, it is only to be expected that one day the retort come back that thin pursed lips are in fact ugly and ungraceful. Up to now, because Whites were considered the norm, the Black becomes the non-normal; thus, any judgment, however veiled, per force privileges Whites. When the day comes when Black people decide that they are for themselves their own canon of beauty, the White as model will become obsolete and even inferior. Let us then only wish for that other day to arrive when the existence of many such canons can be embraced, each admirable in its own context.

It is thus very important to recognize one remarkable fact: *difference is always a double-entry ledger.* For the European immigrants in America, the Indians were "redskins," but for the Indians, the Europeans were "palefaces." Men judge women to be fragile, clumsy, and inefficient; women judge masculinity to be brutal and boorish. Who is right? Evidently, both and neither. The same holds for the egotistical myopia of majoritarian thinking; it doesn't see that its misestimation of and contempt for the minority is mutual. If a difference has become privileged, it is through the law of the conqueror, imposed by force. The real evil is that, when interiorized by the vanquished, it becomes the only recognized law.[41] Little thought is given to the fact that for a Black man, Black women might be the most beautiful of women, and that for the Eskimo, the Eskimo child is the most beautiful baby in the world. When the Bible speaks of unquestionable beauty, it says, "beautiful like an Ethiopian"; what this signifies is that Ethiopia was once a powerful empire. Since then, Black people have been downtrodden everywhere. To legitimate slavery, it was necessary to denigrate their particular physiognomy. Everything revolves around this central idea; from this comes the real or pretended sexual prowess of Black people, their real or imagined special odor. Redheads would have been devalorized if redheaded people had been made slaves; had redheaded people been the masters, they would have been the ones devalorizing White and Brown people.

... and the Confirmations of Experience

Concomitant with these illustrations and verifications from the mouths of the oppressed of what I had been thinking, fate also provided more experiential testimony.

The MRAP, a movement struggling against racism, sought to give its activities a more solid foundation; it sought to develop concrete rather than merely polemical arguments. Its leadership decided to undertake a survey of racism in France and asked me if I would help in the project. I accepted. Since it would require more than one person to do the work, I invited the excellent sociologist Paul H. Maucorps to participate, and he, in turn, brought in a team of enthusiastic young researchers. We set to work.

We immediately confronted a minor embarrassment. To economize on funds that, for MRAP, were limited, we had to disseminate our questionnaire through the organization's journal. The readers of this weekly magazine were all, a priori, anti-racist. The project must then proceed from a paradox: in order to study racism, we would have to address people who condemned it. And who were unhappy about doing it for us, besides. But upon reflection, we decided we could use even this paradox. If these presumed anti-racists let slip any racist sentiments in their responses, it would certainly suggest a fortiori how deeply rooted racist attitudes were. And it was well we did: the results by and large demonstrated exactly that. (For the most part, it was a survey of opinion; no one, except in some very rare cases, admitted to being racist, having to address someone who would read their response.)

The report we drew up after analyzing the survey had the usual faults of the genre; it was at once too detailed and too opaque. But the descriptions and correlations it established, the conclusions that we thought warranted reporting, remain valid still. The flatness and the minutiae of the data allowed us to circumscribe various different signs of racist manifestation—opinions, attitudes, conduct—and to relate them to different oppressed groups: Jews, Arabs, Blacks, Gypsies, and so on. We were also careful to relate the returns to the time and place they were produced.

This project confirmed my original hypotheses: *beyond variations with respect to different dominant/dominated pairs, that is, of racist attitudes and their particular victims, the general mechanism of racist thinking was shown to be fairly similar over an entire sample.* Under the circumstances, this applied to

France, across the diverse groups that compose it, and across the different situations in which racism manifested itself.

I have not conducted similar surveys in other countries, but what I know of Black Americans, of colonized people of the Maghreb, and of the Quebecois suggests to me that the results would not be terribly different. My friends entrusted to me particularly the drafting of the introduction and the conclusion to our report. In writing it, I started by recalling the general structure I had theorized and enlarged it in terms of what we learned from the survey.

DEFINITION

The unfolding of a thought does not always resemble that of life. Were things to happen the way they should, the outcome of these long researches and theorizations should have been definitive. As it is, I have had to put these studies together in several different ways. When Lucie Faure, the editor of *Le Nef*,[1] asked me to collaborate on a special issue on racism, I jumped at the chance and wrote the article "Racism: An Attempt at a Definition." I reviewed the four points developed in *The Colonizer and the Colonized*, which were further elaborated in *Portrait of a Jew*, and added a commentary on each point, term by term, in the manner of Spinoza. I proposed this essay as a working hypothesis for the MRAP survey. Later, I incorporated it in *Dominated Man*, where, with a conclusion, it served as a kind of conclusion to that book under the subtitle "Racism and Oppression" [see Appendix A, "An Attempt at a Definition"].

The article "Racism" that *L'Encyclopaedia Universalis* asked me to write is then the endpoint of this even longer trajectory. It differs quite markedly from the preceding attempts in two important respects [see Appendix B, "What Is Racism?"]. First, it restricts itself to considering racism in the narrow, that is, the biological, sense. It was, I guess, a way of acceding to some objections raised about my earlier thinking. But I still emphatically maintain that *the focus on biological difference, despite its shrillness, at least among our contemporaries, is not the essential aspect of racism.* It is, rather, merely a pretext or an alibi. However, something is to be gained by distinguishing the strictly biological dimension of racist thinking from others. That is what I did in that article.

The second point of the encyclopedia article concerned the function of racism. What I have tried to demonstrate, beyond the rage or hystrionics of the racist outlook, beyond its incoherences and contradictions, is that *racism has a function.* It is both the emblem and the rationalization for a system of social oppression. Should a definition of racism include reference to the systematicity of domination through the advantages it purveyed, given that it seeks to be as concise as possible? Ultimately, I decided that it should. Moreover, I thought it would not be too difficult—essentially a question of formulation, to which I will return in a moment. But I have never wavered on what I consider the most fundamental aspect: *the organic connection between racism and oppression.*

I maintain that racism, and the general structure that underlies it and of which it is a particular case, summarizes and symbolizes what I have previously addressed about the systematicity of social oppression. In other words, racism subsumes and reveals all the elements of dominance and subjection, aggression and fear, injustice and the defense of privilege, the apologetics of domination with its self-justifications, the disparaging myths and images of the dominated, and finally the social destruction or social nullification of the victimized people for the benefit of their persecutors and executioners—all this is contained in it. Assuming, of course, that one sees a general structure underneath the unfolding of racist practices. This is not a circular argument in which I require that one accept in advance what I claim to be demonstrating; it is rather a question of an articulation that will encompass the greatest number of cases.

Broad Sense and Narrow Sense

Let's step back a bit. Racism in the "strict" or "narrow" sense of the term certainly exists; it is a racism that makes reference to *biological* differences for the purposes of subjugation and the establishment of certain privileges and advantages for itself. There are those who believe they can compile sets of such traits to form coherent paradigms, which they call *races*. For them, the other races will be those that are impure and abominable, and their own, pure and admirable. By authorizing this peculiar superiority for themselves, they also presume to enjoy advantages of a different order: economic or political, for example, or perhaps psychological, or simply a measure of prestige.

But a broader use of the term *racism* also undeniably exists—though, perhaps, pushing the term to its limit—in which the persecutor evinces the same attitude in the name of nonbiological differences (regardless of whether there are biological differences or not). The same processes of self-valorization through the devaluation of the other are at work, to the same end of justifying forms of verbal or physical assault and abuse. Furthermore, one cannot really interpret the first without understanding the second. And since the second is more common than the first, it would seem reasonable to consider biological racism, which is a relatively recent phenomenon, as a special case of the other, whose practices are more widespread and much older.

In any event, *it should be possible both to distinguish the two senses of racism and to encompass them in one common definition.*

Recalling the Definition

Racist thinking in the narrow sense is that which emphatically focuses on certain biological differences, including those of skin color, the form of the nose, cranial dimensions, curvature of the back, odor, composition of the blood, and even one's posture, one's manner of walking, of looking . . . the list goes on and on. For such racist thinking, these factors all constitute evidence.

Naturally, one can discuss this evidence with those who see it as such, and accuse them of bad faith or defective vision. One can denounce their information as false, or reveal it to be pseudo-knowledge. Usually, it is easy to show the differences to be assumed, or invented, or simply construed to meet the needs of the racist cause. It makes no difference. They will continue to act and to think as if nothing had been said. Indeed, it quickly becomes clear that their focus on either real or imaginary differences is only to provide leverage for other things, namely, to derogate certain other people.

It is thus of the essence of this process that *the other's traits all have a negative valuation.* Whatever they are, they will signify something bad. The correlative effect is that the corresponding characteristics for the one who derogates are good. We must keep this inverse relation in mind; it recurs everywhere, even where not apparent and even where the order of the terms have been changed. What encompasses the core of this relation, whether it be one of dominance-subjection or codependence [*dépendance-pourvoyance,* which would include the dual dependence of the colonial relation], is the notion that the racist and the victimized constitute a structural dyad: the racist is likable because the victim is detestable; the world of the racist is moral while the world of the victim is evil.

A pragmatic conclusion that people who think in a racist manner arrive at and believe legitimate is that they have to protect themselves, and protect their own, against contamination by this evil and against the potential (imminent) aggression of the other—to the point of needing to attack first. The Jews have quick fingers, sticky palms, and a ferret's nose, all of which point to their ability to sniff out money; therefore, one becomes an anti-Semite to defend oneself against them. Compared to Whites, Black people have an unnatural erotic power; *therefore,* in order to protect White women and the entire White race against them, lynchings become necessary.

The relative (structural) coherence of racism in the narrow sense, even in its obsessive aggressiveness and self-interest, *is confirmed precisely by the existence of racism in the broad sense.* I must mention that, ironically, while I have never seen the narrow definition seriously contested, though it is founded on biological differences that are themselves often neglected, many people have indignantly rejected the broad definition, though it holds the key to understanding the former.

In terms of the broad definition, I have still only scratched the surface. The discriminatory dyadic relations of social ostracism, which provide the machinery for real, concrete social exclusion, are found in many other forms of human relations, where biological considerations are either absent or irrelevant. They participate in obscure domains where fear and aggression dominate, where fear leads to aggression, and where aggression gives rise to more fear. Indeed, in a more exact sense, fear leads to aggression, aggression engenders more aggression, and that aggression provokes more fear. It is an endless circle that lives by feeding off itself. That is why it does not matter if one describes racism in terms of fear or aggression. Each engenders the other, like the chicken and the egg. *Racists are people who are afraid*; they feel fear because they attack, and they attack because they feel fear. They are afraid of being attacked, or they are afraid because they believe themselves attacked and attack to rid themselves of this fear. But why is there a fear of being attacked? Generally, it is because one wishes to obtain or defend something of value. I have already spoken of the many forms in which value can clothe itself. Whatever its form, however, and regardless of whether the threat is real or imaginary, the necessity to defend an individual identity and a collective identity, against all who come from elsewhere and don't belong, is in operation. But defensiveness requires an offense, and vice versa; then, having become aggressive, one awaits retaliation. Fear feeds fear and aggression feeds aggression. But underneath it all, *racial affirmation is an instrument for self-affirmation*. It is a detestable way of binding the social body together, through the self-exaltation of specific traits in order to debase others correlatively, but only one among many. It is no accident that nationalism, for instance, transforms itself so often into chauvinism; it is itself already a hostile denigration of other nations.

On the other hand, narrow racial arguments, which do not have a good reputation, are very often voluntarily abandoned. It does not mean that racist thinking has become less pernicious or denigratory toward others; the bigot will not deprive himself of an attack on fellow humans, if one can put it that way. Instead, racist thinking finds plenty of other "noxious" differences with which to reproach others. Psychology, culture, social customs and institutions, even metaphysics furnish many opportunities for defamation. One no longer detests Arabs because they have a swarthy complexion or a Levantine physiognomy but because they practice ("let us admit it") a ridiculous religion, they treat their women badly, and they are cruel, or simply retarded. Okay, so not all Jews resemble the Wandering Jew, nor are they quick-fingered or hook-nosed, but "you must recognize" that they are in general greedy, cosmopolitan, given to treachery, and even, as the evangelists have said, capable of sacrificing God. Granted, neither the Germans nor the English nor the Italians have a distinct physical character (although, for the Italians . . .). But in every German you know a Prussian sleeps, and now it is an industrial Prussian bent on dominating Europe; in every Englishman, there is an unscrupulous adversary who has never renounced domination of the seas, or the subjugation of France, in a nation that now, in the Common Market, thinks only of its own interests (as if the other partners are doing something else). As for the poor Italians, there is only pandemonium, cowardice, and thievery—look at the tragic and ridiculous Red Brigades. Let us add the Japanese (who now comport themselves as industrial nations always have, but then, times also change: the colonial nations used to use force without hesitation—look at the Opium Wars). And even the Arabs, who wish to impose their price! (As all monopolists have always done.) All this signifies, at the same time, that the French are humanist, prudent, loyal, generous (often to a fault, but it is only an excess of quality!), properly organized (not too much, like the Germans, or too little, like the Italians), courageous (unlike the Italians), and not regimented (like the Prussians). . . . One has only to take the contrary of any of the aberrant traits of others to arrive at the positive portrait of the French created by themselves.

Naturally, this double description can be redrawn from anyone else's perspective. Everyone has a stock of self-satisfying images of himself or herself along with unflattering ones of others. (Conversely, in each of us, as individuals or groups, there also exist self-denigrating or even self-destructive attitudes, discourses, and behaviors, but to address that would be to digress from our subject.) And all such images are mutually contradictory. It is all what should induce a modicum of modesty, if not a prudent irony about oneself and about humanity. But for that, one would need the imagination and will to put oneself in another's shoes. That is, one would have to stop being racist, since racism is precisely not doing so, and taking sides with inequality. It doesn't matter if, within each discriminatory dyad, the characteristics listed actually form a coherent whole or not. Being rational is not the issue; a different sort of logic is at work, the logic of fear and obsession.

In short, if I do not wish to omit consideration of those who practice the same discriminatory exclusions without using the biology alibi, I must recognize the existence of a *general structure,* which traditional racism resembles like a son his father but which subsumes racism and generalizes it. A more open definition that takes into account all the alibis, the biological as well as the others, becomes necessary.

Thus, we arrive at the following. *Racism is a generalizing definition and valuation of differences, whether real or imaginary, to the advantage of the one defining and deploying them* [accusateur], *and to the detriment of the one subjected to that act of definition* [victime], *whose purpose is to justify (social or physical) hostility and assault* [agression].

A definition, of course, if I may be forgiven for repeating myself (see *Dependence*), is only a tool, an operational formula. If it is too general, it falls short of its purpose; by attempting to cover too broad a terrain, it grasps nothing adequately. But if too narrow, it will leave out of account too much of what it intended to circumscribe. I do not know how to make this one more concise, nor do I think it needs to be further developed. I have attempted to include a maximum of meaning in a minimum of words. What is important is that the essential idea not be lost to a concern for elegance and that it not be transformed into description through wordiness. I do not pretend that all the problems inherent in this subject are here dispensed with, but I think that this definition has what is needed to resolve them.

The main objections to this definition all boil down to this: in its broadness, it risks diluting the specificity of the racist arguments and dismisses the particularity of racism in its deployment of race and of the biological. But objectively, that is not the case. Many people speak and conduct themselves in a racist manner but claim innocence when accused of it. In any case, there is an easy solution to the problem: two formulations of the same definition, one concerning racism in the strict biological sense and the other addressing all the other forms.

And here, by good fortune, the god of language comes to my rescue. The whole thing revolves around and resolves itself through the biological term; it is sufficient to add or subtract it to obtain a narrow or a broad formulation, without changing anything else. Thus, in its narrow form, it would be: "Racism is the valuation of *biological differences,* real or imaginary . . ." In its broad form: "Racism is the valuation of *differences,* real or imaginary . . ."

Others have suggested condensing the definition even more. I admit I have not found them convincing. I thought for a moment of paring it down to *racism is the refusal of the other.* This is true but inadequate to the point of being false. On the one hand, indifference is a form of refusal, and on the other, not all refusal is aggressive or denigrating. I can refuse someone while fully admitting his superiority, on one plane if not on all. There are people who do not like Jews, while fully granting them recognition as people. There are ways in which compliments given to those victimized by racism can be very subtly poisoned; for example, some say that Jews are *too* intelligent (in order not to denigrate); or that Levantines (Arabs from the Eastern Mediterranean) are exaggeratedly friendly (rather than call them cunning). Of course, it is sometimes difficult not to reveal a certain animosity in one's refusal, but one is not obliged to love everyone. That would be an admirable ideal, but the issue here is that of harming people. Yet while all racism is harmful through its hostility, the inverse is not true; not all aggression is racist. To strike out at an antagonist, even preemptively, is not necessarily a sign of racism; one can respect and admire an adversary. Racism arises from a certain motivation; it utilizes particular mental procedures, from a very clear social motivation. It is not even enough to say that it is an aggressive refusal of the other; it is an aggressive refusal for a particular end, which is justified by a specific type of discourse. A definition must take account of this complexity; to overly impoverish its wording would be to lose its specific insight.

Similarly, with respect to the goals of racism, two formulations, a narrow one and a broad one, are possible, distinguished by whether one focuses on racism's assaultiveness in general or on its effects, that is, on the modes of control and privilege produced. Usually, something does not appear as a privilege unless it is lived as an injustice or a deprivation by others, by those less privileged. A benefit accruing to all people would have no need of justification. A mode of control is not experienced as bad unless it is resented as being concretely oppressive. If one's questioning proceeds only to the level of the "how" of racism, the answer is through hostility and aggression. But one can also ask "why" there is aggression; racism is aggression motivated either by the fear of losing something one possesses or by the fear of an adversary whom one wants to exploit to one's own advantage, and whom one then has to dominate for that purpose. In short, it is in defense of a real or potential benefit.

In any case, the duality of fear and aggression, if it really is a duality, is integral to the structure of all racist practices. Fear always accompanies the undertaking of hostility. To dispense with fear in confidence, the adversary or victim would have to be presumed so totally disarmed that there was no risk. For racism, its attacks are always seen as preventive reactions to what is unforeseeably foreseen as aggression by the adversary.[2] And fear is always a factor in one form or another. There is fear because one is preparing to attack the other, and there is fear of the other. One fears those who are unknown; one fears that they may be violent and invade; one fears that they will take away what one has of value, whether real or symbolic. "They want to take over everything." "They will take our women and our daughters." "We can no longer feel at home here."

The sense of threat can be yet more subtle than that. When I was correcting the proofs of this book, an association of specialized educators approached me with a problem: they asked if I thought there was a close relation between racism and the attitudes that so-called normal people often held toward those who were physically or mentally handicapped. I answered yes, that I thought so. One finds, at least at first sight, a similar sense of rejection out of fear, sometimes a pattern of hostile defensiveness, and even a secret desire to do away with the handicapped. Here again, it would be clear what passage to the limit would mean; the Nazis also tried to exterminate the mentally ill. I am not sure that euthanasia does not partially derive from a similar disaffection. Indeed, the special rehabilitation centers into which people injured in auto accidents have been placed seem motivated by the same feeling; there, they can live with each other but out of our sight. Why such ostracism? Perhaps because they present an image that upsets our own psychic equilibrium—which would amount to the loss of a very precious possession.

Parenthetically, let me add a word of caution. I am not trying to point an accusatory finger. On the contrary, the sense of being obscurely disturbed, as a sensitivity, can actually be of great assistance in caring for the disabled. In other words, a fearful malaise, though it may be an inherent ingredient in racist behavior, does not in itself constitute racism. Racism truly begins when one prepares or justifies an offense or an assault through the devaluation of the other; that is, when one sets in motion certain discursive machinery that conceptually nullifies others and whose main function is to provide the groundwork for concretely preying upon and injuring them.

In truth, the single difficulty that surpasses the problem of formulation is knowing whether a real form of privilege is at issue. The question is crucial, since it governs all the rest. If there is profit to be gained, or benefits to be defended, then a form of racism is possible. And, on that basis, I think my affirmative answer was correct.

If we now look at the case of the rich, of those who want for nothing, there is clearly privilege. Yet still, just to be on the safe side, let us see what its limits might be. As previously stated, there is privilege only when there is consciousness of an injustice. A person who is privileged, yet wholly convinced of his or her rights to this privilege, should feel no need to be racist. Similarly, an individual or a group that had no doubts concerning itself or its domination of others should feel no need to justify itself. Racism would be of no use. In fact, some people have actually told me of certain colonists who, feeling secure in the legitimacy of colonialism, evince none of the reactionary behavior that I have attributed to them. Maybe. Personally, I have never encountered it. What I have encountered are endless attempts at justification, with greater or lesser self-assurance, accompanied by always self-legitimizing disparagements of the colonized. One of the greatest French sociologists, Roger Bastide, told me that the bourgeoisie of Europe was not racist. The proof was their cosmopolitanism and the facility with which they, following the example of royalty, contracted mixed marriages. I remain unconvinced. Neither cosmopolitanism nor exogamic marriages have ever obviated xenophobia. Let us say that, in their given situation, they could afford to grasp the relativity of peoples and cultures, and thus were harder to deceive. *Racism is also a self-deception.* One must be seriously fooled about oneself, as well as about others, to believe in one's essential superiority or in one's overweening rights. And racist thinking always contains a sense of superiority founded upon the hierarchy it establishes between itself and those it racializes as other. It is the hierarchy, though not the superiority, that is real because racism bestows *objective advantages*. As a White person, one can be crippled, miserable, or dim-witted and still believe oneself superior to all Black people—or, as a European, to all Arabs—though the other be rich, handsome, and well educated. Now one would suppose, for the rich who want for nothing, that their own discursive violence, and the racism that would flow from it, would be inversely proportional to their confidence in their own thinking—a correlation that is in itself interestingly instructive.

In contrast, since privileges do exist and are perceived and lived as such, even though relative and at times somewhat ridiculous, various compensatory mechanisms come into play. "The natives have gotten what they deserve," one of our professors at the Lycée Carot de Tunis repeated endlessly. Though he was an upstanding man, all things considered, he reaped some small benefit from colonialism and did not manage to grasp his complicity in it. "These people are lazy, liars, incapable of good farming, only good enough for 'Arab-work,'" he would say, "whereas the workers of my country . . ." Then, without fear of contradiction, speaking of those same workers in "his country," he revealed that he thought still less well of them: "They should have gotten in on the colony!" "They too would have had a share in colonization." But, he fumed with enormous contempt, "They prefer the filth of their small lives to that of adventure." We began to understand that whatever benefits he got, he felt he had merited them because he had taken the leap and the risk. If the others, the inferior ones, the natives, the workers, lived in misery, it was their own fault. The memory of such talk helped me later when writing *The Colonizer and the Colonized.*

The Racism of the Impoverished

One last question: can there be a racism of the dominated? I have already responded in the affirmative, but I think that one can even distinguish two varieties. The first, of course, is that toward those who are more impoverished—and there are always those who are worse off than oneself. I describe this *pyramid of tyrannies* with respect to colonial society, for which it constitutes a skeleton (see *The Colonizer and the Colonized*). Ultimately, I think it can be found everywhere. There are, for instance, those astonishing stories of certain communist-led municipal administrations that evicted North African workers from the city with extraordinary brutality. Two accusations were immediately levied: first, that it was an election-oriented stratagem, and second, that it was just plain racism. The two charges are not in close accord. If this were a calculated election strategy, then it is not done out of conviction. If it is done out of conviction, it is not just an electoral strategy, which would be contingent. I do not believe that the French communists became racists all of a sudden. But it might be more serious than that. As informed politicians, who know their constituencies well, *what they expressed was the potential racism of their electorate.* One has but to review the justifications they gave for their actions: young couples, they explained, can no longer find residence in the public housing projects; there is no more room for the children of workers in the school complexes, and those children increasingly speak bad French because of contact with the children of foreigners; the immigrants make too much noise in the street at night; their cooking smells up the stairwells of the buildings; they play their music too loud; they break everything, and so on (as if French cooking had no odors and disco music was boring and noninvasive). Too often this is how French workers characterize North Africans. The crime of the communists is to have made use of these unfortunately too real sentiments. In 1977, a Harris poll showed that the hostility against the Jews and against the North Africans in France was found principally among workers and retirees. But why do French workers think this way? It is because French workers think that immigrants threaten the few advantages that they have over them. The fear of unemployment, for example, is not unrelated to this hostility. However impoverished one may be, one's poverty can always be less than that of another, at least in other domains.

More to the point, the workers who possess this attitude are the workers who live in daily contact with the immigrants, and not the inhabitants of the nicer neighborhoods; again, difference disquiets, and the oppressed do not escape that malaise. Nevertheless, we have recently witnessed an extraordinary upheaval of a similar nature in a town just outside Paris that was not confined to the working class. The Moslem immigrants there wanted to build a mosque. Though they had been tolerated when unnoticed, they were found intolerable the moment they decided their residence was to be permanent and henceforth marked by a large fancy stone structure, accompanied by the strange songs of the *muezzin*. Let it be said, in passing, that this event elicited the claim from many that they had a high tolerance threshold, which others characterized more justly as an intolerance threshold. It was as if the issue were like an illness induced by the concentration of some toxic agent in the social body, except that the Moslem population would not change in number or in nature with the building of the mosque. In other words, the illness was not in those attacked (the Moslems) but in their detractors, who thus reveal their latent racism.

Is there, then, a racism of the impoverished against the rich? I suppose I may shock some people by answering in the affirmative. But it is a racism that is in part reactive, though it obeys the same mechanism as the other. Take a look at Epinal's cartoon images of the possessing classes, capitalists and small proprietors; they are presumed to be perverse and deformed, that is to say, evil and biologically corrupt. Let us add, the bourgeoisie is universally suspect a priori of these two characteristics, which we have noted in all cases of racism. From the steel-mill owner to the petty bourgeoisie of the nineteenth century, through the large and small entrepreneurs of our day, all are considered avaricious and cruel, afflicted with an unbridled sexuality that threatens the daughters of the people. Antithetically, the poor man, the proletarian, is good, healthy, and virtuous. Here again is the old seesaw movement: differences (perhaps biological, perhaps imaginary) are set in relief for the purpose of self-valorization and in order to devalue the other. And on the horizon lurks the justification of an eventual attack, both individual ("all bosses are the enemy") and collective (the necessity of revolution).

If the racism of the poor gets less notice, it is because they have an excuse. Too often plundered, and sometimes crushed, they are precluded from many pleasures of life, barred from the objects of their desire, of which they dream more avidly because it is denied them. How could they not be full of bitterness and resentment against those whom they believe are the cause of their situation? And who in fact are most often. In addition, because the troubled souls of the downtrodden are scarcely noticed, it is only through the violence of revolutionary upheavals or impulsive individual acts, for which they are severely punished, that the poor can express themselves. In confrontation with the dominant, the racism of the dominated remains at the level of opinion. *The racism of the poor is ordinarily a toothless racism*—except when it manifests itself against other poor people.

Generalization[3]

The mutable character of the racist phenomenon repeats itself everywhere one turns. If I do not always mention this facet, here or in other places, it is because it appears to me to go without saying.[4] But I definitely think that racism's plasticity is an essential part of its nature. One sees this in operation in two of its other facets: *the tendency to generalize and the tendency toward absoluteness.*

There are times when these two aspects of racist valuation of the other are not wholly evident. Sometimes it may look as if a person is simply heaping opprobrium on another individual, without allusion to the person's group or status. But I think one would find a double generalization implicit if one scratches the surface. First, an act of disparagement almost always implicitly refers at least in part to a group, in the sense that others must also suffer from the quality being disparaged. And second, the content of what is said tends to be atemporal, that is, not a function of time; no foreseeable event will ever put an end to it.

To say that a certain Black worker cannot master a technique because he is Black is to say that no Black person can do it; therefore, all Blacks, or almost all, are technologically inferior. To describe a woman as having "long hair and short ideas" because she is a woman designates all other women as well. When a bigoted person is obliged to recognize the professional, artistic, or scientific merits of a particular woman, he tends to twist that recognition to fit his own logic; "it is the exception that proves the rule."

Socialization

The tendency to generalize is sustained by the underlying *sociality of racism* to the point where it becomes difficult to address its generalizations because they are themselves so universally generalized throughout society—that is, they go without saying. Though racism has some roots in a person's emotional structure and sensibilities, its basic formulation is social. *Racism is a cultural discourse* that surrounds each person from childhood on, in the air one breathes, in parental advice and thinking, in one's cultural rituals. One is exposed to it in school, in the streets and the newspapers, even in the writings of people one is supposed to admire and who might be otherwise admirable. Remarks have been made by Voltaire, Balzac, and Gide that reveal their repulsion of Jews. The Jew, the Arab, the Black, and even the Corsican, the Italian, and the German have become literary or cinematic stereotypes, through which they eventually are treated as cartoon characters themselves. Racist or chauvinist vocabulary becomes the reservoir, the social memory of a group's hostility toward others: for the Arab, *le raton, le melon, le bougnoul*; for the Jew, *le youpin, le judas, le moise*; for the Italian, *le rital, le macaroni, le spaghetti*; for the German, *le boche, le frisé, le schleuh, le mangeur de choucroute.*[5] It is remarkable how lively verbal invention becomes when it concerns social prejudice. A veritable fireworks of derogatory terms exploded on us during the Algerian War, as did anti-German nicknames during the Second World War. These derogatory terms actually define, concretize, and nourish one's individual experiences. *Racism is a collective language at the service of each person's emotions.*

Racist practices are doubly socialized in both their discursivity and their purpose. *It is a discourse formulated by a group that addresses itself to a group*. At the level of these totalizations, the function of racism becomes clearer still. An individual is no longer considered in himself but rather as a member of a social group, whose characteristics he possesses a priori. Through an individual, an entire group can be stigmatized as detestable and offensive, and condemned to being attacked; inversely, each individual member of a group so stigmatized will be seen as warranting denigration and hostility, a priori. When the racist recognizes any good qualities in a particular group member, it is with regret or astonishment. "There are good people everywhere," he will claim, meaning, "even in your group, otherwise so contemptible." Or, more to the point, "you are not like the others"; "I have a friend who is Jewish and who . . . ," which hardly praises the others who are not exempt from the usual derogation and its eventual "punitive violence." Besides, even for "the exceptions that prove . . . ," the suspension of judgment is only temporary. At the slightest mistake, the least social impropriety, the alleged misunderstanding is dispelled, and the guilty one again becomes what he had always been, a member of an abominable group. "At bottom, they are all alike." The suspicion had never totally disappeared. It was simply put on the back burner, masked by a provisional indulgence in favor of "someone who does not merit it"—again, a priori. What had happened "shows that only too well."

These uses of generalization represent another way the racist proclaims reason to be on his side. "You see? What did I tell you?" "I knew that he was no good." Things are put back on track. The systematic hostility of the racist turned out to be an asset, keeping him always on guard with respect to necessarily deplorable people; with it, one runs no risk of being taken in or taken by surprise. Thus, if he considers every Gypsy to be a potential thief, he warns against this Gypsy here, because "forewarned is forearmed." No matter that *this* Gypsy has done nothing. If he wished to commit a theft, it would have been forestalled in advance. It is a measure of security, a practical and logical guarantee that both protects and completes the racist's argument. In the meanwhile, this Gypsy, who is not a thief, neither in act nor in intention, is truly treated as one. But that doesn't bother the racist; it is precisely what it means to be a racist.

The other totalizing dimension is that of *extension in time*. It follows in the footsteps of social generalization. Racism seeks to render definitive the stereotype that it attaches to the other. Not only does the other belong to a group of which all the members are rotten, but they will be that way *forever.* Thus, all is in order for eternity. The bad guys are the way they are *definitively,* and the good guys as well—the masters on one side, the slaves on the other. That a Black person fails to master the technique only signifies that he never has been able to and never will. Similarly for the colonized: they have never understood industrialization, science, or progress, and they therefore never will . . . until decolonization.

Once again, it corroborates the expedience of the biological argument. The inferiority of the colonized, of the Black, or of the woman is inscribed in their flesh. "How one might wish that it were otherwise, and could be corrected, but it is their destiny." And what destiny is more tenacious than the biological? The Black is irremediably black; the woman irremediably female. *Biology is the very figure of fate.* The prey of the racist was predisposed in his or her being and condemned to remain like that until the end of time. And what better guarantee of privilege is there than eternity? Thus, these social and temporal totalities are transformed directly into metaphysical assurance. It is truly a passage to the absolute. The Jew, the Black, the Arab, the Gypsy, even the woman, become figures of irremediable evil. The Jew, as the accursed elect of God, author of the death of God, remains outside time and disturbs both the moral and the cosmic order. Has it not been suggested, seriously, that the Black recalls by his color the darkness of malevolence itself? And then there is the figure of Lilith, Eve's double, the one born of sperm, the inconsummate actress, ancestor of the *femme fatale*, the devourer of man, whose infernal appetite is as much for money as it is for sex. Racism reaches its apogee in metaphysics and in religion; do not the metaphysicians and theologians see themselves as specialists of the eternal? But here, it is a question of a negative absolute.

Negation and Nullification

We can now see, in passing, how social negation is the prelude to social nullification. How much is conscious and how much unconscious can be debated. The moderate racist, if one can use such a term, would probably be horrified if he took full account of where the path of racism leads—to the cemetery. Yet it is never a question of anything but the ongoing process, more or less hidden, more or less affirmed, of symbolic destruction whose end is the dehumanization of its victim. There are racists who have no desire to see a Black person or a colonized person suffer a violent death. It would not be a fitting end for someone they instead consider rather comic. But the actual death or suffering of such a person provokes in them a sense of derision rather than compassion. The one who suffers is not exactly a human being, with a mother and children, but rather a species of animal, and it is always easier to imagine the disappearance, even the eradication, of animals than of humans. The moment at which Black people began to be thought of in this fashion can be dated precisely: it was the period of the slave trade in Africans. I strongly suspect that such were the sentiments, perhaps not wholly conscious, of many people when they learned of the systematic massacres of Indian tribes throughout the Americas—a massive entrapment of beasts in the form of humans. But sometimes the blatant desire for murder also gets expressed. How often have I heard, in the colonies, the gratuitous remark that tries to be a pleasantry:

"We are 10 percent of the population; give each of us a rifle and nine bullets, and the problem will be solved."

What provides the key to the violence in racist discourse is a psychological inversion—one accuses the victim of absolute evil because one wishes an absolute evil upon him. The Jew is accused of murder because one wishes him dead. (The syllogism "He poisons the wells; should he then not die?" is a reformulation of the real thought: I want him to die, so I accuse him of poisoning the wells.) "The Black is the power of the infernal; should he not be sent there?" is a translation of its real inverse: I wish him in hell, so I consider him a creature escaped from there. It is fortunate that all exclusions do not end in such extremes. But there is more than enough historical experience to convince us that the difference between the stigmatization of the other and, when sufficiently critical circumstances arise, his or her physical destruction is not a difference of kind but of degree.[6] Not so long ago in Europe the background social atmosphere of misogyny was transformed into mass suffering through the stoning to death or burning at the stake of women as witches.

Racism and Heterophobia

Finally, let me say one more word about terminology, recognizing that no attempt to clarify language can fail to influence our vocabulary. The ambiguity in any discussion of racism derives in part from the ambiguity of the word. In its strict sense, racism refers exclusively to a biological concept. But then, through its use, it comes to have a much broader meaning. Many people no longer think of biology at all when they speak in a racist manner. That does not mean they are making a mistake, however, since both uses have a common source.

To resolve the ambiguity, could there not be two terms marking the duality, but sufficiently close to suggest their common source? Can one not express the disparity in the double definition by means of a linguistic distinction? Here is what I suggest.

The word *racism* works perfectly well for the biological notion. But I propose that henceforth it be limited to that. This would not stop current racist discourse from sailing along as always in fact and fantasy, but it would at least provide an instrument better suited to dealing with it. When one speaks of racism, the term would refer to people who accord primacy to biological characteristics. There would be less time wasted making arguments that do not address the essential question. Many people who think and act in terms that are exclusionary or derogatory insist that they do not do so in the name of biological concepts. It would be unjust not to take note of this, let alone unveil their latent racism, if it exists.

I think that the word *heterophobia* would work well enough to refer to these people. Heterophobia would designate the many configurations of fear, hate, and aggressiveness that, directed against an other, attempt to justify themselves through different psychological, cultural, social, or metaphysical means, of which racism in its biological sense is only one instance. To my knowledge, this term does not exist in the dictionary, but perhaps need and usage will change that. Many people think themselves cleansed of the sin of racism if they pay little attention to skin color, to the form of the nose or the size of the lips. But are they less guilty if they attack others for their religious faith, or for cultural differences?

The term *heterophobia* would be relevant as well to more recent issues. It is questionable whether one could speak of racism with respect to prejudice against teenagers, or women, or gay men and lesbians, or the handicapped. Strictly speaking, it wouldn't apply—although either in irony or in confirmation of the importance of difference, little attention has been paid to the fact that for both women and teenagers, real though not racial biological differences exist. A man I know once said of my friends, with questionable humor, "I do not know if there is a Jewish race, but the women, now that is truly a race apart!" Naturally, the compliment would have worked as well if spoken by his wife with respect to the men. And in that sense, for adults, teenagers are quasi-biologically different. The term *heterophobia* would allow one to encompass all these varieties of hostility and exclusion. Inversely, it has the advantage of modifiability to fit different cases. For example, instead of speaking of anti-Semitism, which is manifestly imprecise, one might employ the term *Judeophobia,* which clearly signifies both fear and hostility toward Jews. The same can be said for *Negrophobia* and *Arabophobia.* I leave to the reader the pleasure of searching for terms that would represent the hostile fear and devaluation of women or adolescents, of homosexuals or old people, and so on.[7]

One last word on this subject. I am not wedded to these distinctions, any more than I am to the wording of a definition. I simply see a need for a definition that can operate at two levels at once and that thus calls for a corresponding double terminology. The details can be discussed. I once gave some thought to the adjectival part; it occurred to me that *alterophobia* would work as well as *heterophobia.* I abandoned it out of a certain purism; "altero-" comes from Latin, and "phobia" from Greek. Though we should be accustomed to such things—the term "socio-logy," for instance—I thought that in making something new, one should attempt to make it better. There is also *ethnophobia,* which has the advantage of referring to the exclusion of a group as a whole, one of the central characteristics of racist practice. But to insist on this generalized character exclusively risks being restrictive in turn. Racist speech can be addressed to a singular individual, even were it to submerge him or her in the plural later on. The same goes for *xenophobia,* which has the virtue of existing already and, through its etymological roots, would have been adequate. But usage is king: the term *xenophobia* refers exclusively to the exclusion and denigration of foreigners. Not only foreigners are excluded, unless what is understood by "foreigner" is all who are different from us—by age, sex, social class—but that would stretch the meaning of the word too much.

Enough on this point. I persist in proposing the

pair *racism* and *heterophobia*. The first designates the refusal or rejection of the other in the name of biological differences; the second the rejection of the other in the name of no matter what difference. The second includes the first as a special case. And what I have tried to do here is come up with a single definition that would be unitary and at the same time able to articulate this duality.[8]

TREATMENT

It is not required of an author that he provide the practical applications of his investigations. He himself does not always perceive them. Usually, it takes other, more ingenious minds. But more important, one does not hold his theoretical work responsible if its practical conclusions seem unacceptable. That said, the empirical implications of this work seem obvious and are not wholly discouraging.

THE PHILOSOPHY OF RACISM

What can we conclude from all this? First, the alarming (unconscionable) *banality of racism,* to paraphrase the now-famous expression of Hannah Arendt, who spoke, with respect to the Eichmann trial, of "the banality of evil."[1] And, having brought up that sinister affair, let me add, without digressing too much, that the Nazi death camps were the end result of systematic processes of denigration and social nullification, to which the Jews and other victimized groups had been subjected, which paralleled and reflected, mutatis mutandis, the denial of social being imposed by colonialism on the colonized, and which is found in other forms of oppression. History provides many other examples, each of course with its own specificity. I have been criticized on this score by people who prefer to think that the Nazis were not only unprecedented in human history but also totally bereft of sense. While in solidarity with, and having utmost respect for, all the victims of Nazism and the absolute horror that the Nazi experience meant for them, I do not think that this should prevent our trying to understand the phenomenon.

When the first edition of this book was published in 1982, very little in-depth interpretive work had been done on the subject of the Nazis. This is no longer the case. Research has appeared that gradually sheds light on that phantasmagoric field of ruins, elucidating it little by little. Already, we see certain things more clearly. For instance, contrary to what many wish to believe, the men who, on a racial pretext, carried out the attempted extermination of entire human groups were neither monsters nor insane; they were often just "ordinary men," as the Anglo-Saxon author Christopher Browning put it.[2] Some suffered, some were overcome, some refused, but for most, their roles as executioners became habitual, as the impressive work of Raul Hilberg has shown.[3] It is an unpleasant reality of our species, but a reality nevertheless, and we must consider it carefully if we wish to draw a convincing picture of this horrible past, in order to learn something from it for the future. Indeed, even if we should conclude that it was a kind of dementia, delirium itself has a meaning, and we would still have to decipher it. Dare I suggest that the thesis of absolute unintelligibility is oddly allied with the thesis of absolute yet ungraspable sense—that is, an interpretation that is at once metaphysical and mystical?

One need not rely on such extreme examples, however, to examine the "banality of evil." A while ago, the Parisian journal *Evidences* asked me to analyze some mail that the journal had received in response to a particular television program.[4] It was quite alarming. I would not want to say that all those who wrote about the program were racist. Many strongly condemned racism, and many took actual steps not to succumb to it. But nevertheless, their innocence was rarely pure—the evil came in many guises—and those who protested their virtue only half succeeded. Those who did not attack the Arabs did not succeed in not suspecting the Jews. One who would consent to his daughter's marrying an Arab would hesitate if the future husband were a Black man. Another would let her marry a Jew but surely not an Arab. The reasons given were not all absurd: "It is necessary to take account of the social environment"; "A mixed marriage is full of danger"; "The children of mixed marriages will have more difficulty in life," and so on. Other, less innocent responses were of the sort "I am not racist but . . ."; "Let us recognize, all the same, that the Jews . . ." ". . . that the Gypsies . . . ," proclaimed apparently without suspecting how revealing such disclaimers always are. *The* Jews, *the* Gypsies signify *all* Jews and *all* Gypsies, and reflect therefore a prior condemnation against every individual belonging to the category of Jews or the category of Gypsies.[5] It is another instance of implicit totalization. This matter of the journal's mail occurred before the more methodical survey, "The French and Racism," undertaken for MRAP (see "Description" in this book). Carefully interpreting these spontaneous letters made clear to me that racism is simply not practiced the same way and with the same intensity everywhere but varies with respect to each group chosen for disparagement, as well as at different times and places. Some forms express themselves only in intimate circumstances, while others permit themselves to erupt in public. Some people, while respecting the customs of minorities when practiced in private, will not tolerate their public exhibition. This was seen in the affair of the mosque in the Parisian suburb, and also at a Maghrebian cultural center in Paris. Other people, whether out of cunning or naïveté, claim that they want to protect the marginalized for their own sake and thus counsel discretion (to the people who have been ostracized).[6] In truth, not everyone is racist, and many succeed in defending themselves against it. But recourse to racism is not only easy, it seems so natural; the circumstances simply have to allow it. One could conclude, parodying Descartes, that *the temptation of racism is the most commonly shared thing in the world.*

Why is racism so common? Because it is a very *convenient tool of aggression.*

I have already spoken at length of its expedience, but here are two more examples. I am in the Paris Metro on the Porte de la Chapelle line, with a friend who mentions that its nickname, for those who use it daily, is the "Third World line" or the "Africa-Asia line," because one encounters so many immigrants from those continents on it. Exactly one Black person is in our car; he appears somewhat mentally deranged and is drumming with his hands on the subway seat, on the window, while nodding his head in rhythm. The other riders have that absent air common to subway riders the world over, but they seem a bit anxious about the gestures of this unfortunate man. My friend translates the general sentiment for me. "They are all somewhat odd," she murmurs. I decode what she says: "In other words, he is making these impetuous motions because he is black." If he were white, they would say, he is just a deranged man, but since he is black, they think first of all that here is a Black person. I asked my friend why. She thought seriously about her own reaction and responded in this way. She often takes this subway line, and she always feels a vague anxiety. And today? She admits that she does. And yes, she had thought first of the ethnic origin of our dancer. It is true, it is easy to give in to the temptation to think in biologically racialized terms; the color of the skin, the facial features, the hair all become anchor points for fear, which is then crystalized into hostility.

A second example, again in the Metro: a group of young North Africans loudly invades a subway car. They move around laughing and looking for attention, almost to the point of provocation. My traveling companion, a well-meaning and anti-racist university professor, murmurs uneasily, "They shouldn't do this . . ." I ask him to explain. He tells me that he would like to protect these young people, in some way, from opinion that is already ill disposed toward them. As North Africans, they are suspect in advance. I have previously discussed this "advice" with respect to Jews: "Be discreet, don't call attention to yourselves in a situation already turned against you." My friend recognizes that, in spite of himself, he participates a little in the general sentiment: these are North Africans in Paris; they shouldn't do this. . . . Whatever they do reflects on their status as immigrants. But clearly, here in the subway, it is not just a question of a specifically "North African" mode of behavior: these are adolescents, full of raw excess energy, maladroit in their growing bodies, not yet familiar with all social norms. They seek to dissipate their discomfort in the unwholesome pleasures of intimidating others who are adult, rich, or different, and they are ready for violence should any incident provide the occasion for it. Yet is this not the behavior of any gang of teenage street kids?

I have purposely chosen these two examples because each contains an element of biological difference. The second is more instructive since it contains two differences: age and ethnicity. These North Africans were both North African and younger than the other passengers. The ethnic difference was instinctively chosen as the focus for fear or anxiety, rather than the age difference; the latter would have been adequate but not as opportune, since it would not have enjoyed the more general sense of racialized ill feeling or hostility.

Today, everyone seems to condemn racism. At least, very few proclaim themselves to be racist. Indeed, those who do practice it, whether in word or deed, do not defend it as a *philosophy*.[7] Most often, they explain their gestures and words as arising from something other than racism. One could be content with this, and even reassured, and still seek to understand the nature of the racist phenomenon, even though one's ultimate understanding might be quite disturbing in the end and lead to more than mere indignation. It is necessary to treat racism as a matter of fact, provisionally setting aside all moralism and even, to a certain extent, all preoccupation with action.

From this perspective, we have already discovered a number of aspects that are indeed not reassuring. In light of these, let us allow ourselves to propose some conclusions.[8]

1. *In almost every person there is a tendency toward a racist mode of thinking that is unconscious,* or perhaps partly conscious, or not unconscious at all. From the person who claims, "I am not racist, but . . ." to the one who pretends to recognize Black people by their odor or finds in a Jewish face "the

countenance of the crematorium"; from that uncertain hesitation in one who professes anti-racism to the provocations of the open racist who refuses nothing about racism but the label; from the one who deprecates segregation in America but avoids renting a room to a Black student, to the one who justifies the methods of the Ku Klux Klan and would eventually apply them in France: all propose interpretations and rationalizations for their attitudes and their thinking, but all ultimately share a common denominator. The defender of the KKK proclaims that the sheet-covered Americans only wish to defend their country, the virtue of their women, the color of their children's skin. The one who simply refuses to rent a room to a Black person and admits (or even disapproves) of himself that he feels troubled when he sees a Black man on the street with a White woman also thinks vaguely about the purity of the women and the skin of the future children of the nation.

The interpretations—explanations, disguises, alibis—differ from one to another, but they all go back to the same fact that is at times avowed, at times camouflaged, but always discernible.

2. *Racism, or perhaps I should now say "heterophobia," is ultimately the most widely shared attitude in the world.* That is to say, it is a *social fact*. To a large extent, this explains its importance, its diversity and boundlessness, its profundity and its generality. It preexists and imposes itself on the individual. In other words, before existing at the individual level, racism exists in social institutions and ideologies, in education and culture.

It would be interesting to capture certain cultural aspects of racism on film. I'm thinking, in particular, of how ideologues fabricate ideologies on the basis of relations and institutions of force; of how journalists vulgarize those same ideologies; and how the newspaper reader swallows this diluted poison that, because it is repeated so often, totally infuses his or her consciousness. Not enough has been said about the insidious role of writers and of literature, even the finest, in the propagation of racist themes and images.[9] Nor are religions exempt from the sin of racism. And the family milieu itself is an extraordinary refinery of prejudice, fear, and resentment, from which very few children emerge unscathed. In short, racism is first of all a cultural atmosphere; one breathes it in with the air of the family and the society.

3. Why this generality? Why would so negative an attitude, one so manifestly injurious to ordinary human life, be so fertile?

We promised ourselves to try and understand, and not just reassure ourselves at any price or get indignant at the unprecedented maliciousness of some people. Let us recall: the *racist explanations are expedient.* That is why groups or individuals adopt racism so easily as a stance; it is simply too tempting.

Yet while the racist attitude may be a wholly generalized social fact and easy to come by, it also corresponds to a kind of evidence in which it continually discovers confirmation for itself. *Beyond being a psychological and social fact, racism is also above all an institutional fact.*

The colonized were not simply accused of

being second-class people, they were that in reality. They did not enjoy the same rights as the colonialist. The Black American is not only described as an outsider to White society, he or she is that in most cases. The Jew is really socially separate, more or less discretely segregated (ghettoized).

The inferiorization and debasement of racism's victims are thus describable facts. Then why would one not consider *the racist ideology as an adequate expression of that objective situation*? If the Jews are separate and ghettoized, then something in the Jews, one could say, probably calls for or merits discrimination. If the colonized suffer the crushing and derisive fate that they do, it is because they are colonizable.

Of course, it could be said, to the contrary, that this ideology, the discourse of denigration pushed to the point of myth, both explains and legitimizes the dehumanization to which the oppressed group finds itself subjected. But that would imply, at the same time, accusing oneself, one's own people, and one's own cosmos of having done it. Who is capable of that? It would require a degree of lucidity, of integrity and courage, that few people, even those said to be of high culture, attain. Is it not more "natural," more spontaneous, and much less difficult to look for an explanation that calms one's sense of profound guilt instead, that assuages all individual and group responsibility with respect to the victims of racism?

4. The racist explanation is, on the whole, the most opportune. It is effective, agreeable, even satisfying to the point of euphoria, as the psychologists say. It reassures and it flatters, it excuses and fortifies,

it reinforces one's sense of collective and individual self. Thus, the anxiety and greed of the narcissist who inhabits each one of us is soothed.

And at what a price! Indeed, it makes the others pay! The racist rejoices, justifies, and reassures himself or herself at the expense of others, humiliating them through their otherness. One doesn't even have to take credit for it; the others who are diminished give that credit by proxy. One's superiority does not have to be demonstrated; it is evident in the inferiority of the others.

Racism's allure is that it is the path of least resistance. Why resist a vice whose costs are so minimal? It is a rare vice indeed whose effects are not detrimental to the health of the sinner. This one is always at the expense of the other. Why refuse something so attractive, and so communal as well?

5. To rise in the world, it suffices for one simply to climb on the shoulders of another.

We understand why racist thinking chooses, as the target of its denigrations, those who are already designated as victim; it chooses those who are already resigned, those so subjected to ill treatment that they dare not resist or respond. The ones most victimized are again the ones most convenient, in this great undertaking of convenience. *The racist gravitates by instinct to the most oppressed.* It is easiest to add misfortune to the unfortunate.

One doesn't hear of an anti-American racism, or anti-English, or even anti-German; those are historically strong peoples who are sustained by powerful nations. Racist thinking, in order to savor its "conquest," only attacks people already defeated by History—the weak links in the human chain.

6. That is why the outsider is the target of choice for the racist; the immigrant is always a propitious stepladder for the foot of this mock conqueror. Hence, *the close family resemblance between racism and xenophobia*. The vulnerability of the immigrant calls racism down upon itself, just as disability attracts sarcasm and contempt.

7. Hence, the astonishing racism of the oppressed themselves [see Appendix C, "The Relativity of Privilege"]. The worker, the colonized, the Jew, the Black can all be truly racist in turn. Why would a victimized person attack another in that same way? Simple: for the same reasons as the others and to satisfy the same urges. Upon whom can European workers stand to make themselves a little bigger, if not the immigrant worker, the North African but also the Italian, the Spanish, and even the Polish? That is, even those thought to be of the same race, which proves yet again, if such proof were needed, that racism does not always correspond to race. Over whom can the small colonialist, who is himself exploited and disinherited, aggrandize himself if not on the colonized, whom he can regard from the height of the meager privileges that colonial institutions confer upon him? In the same way, African Americans are tempted to disparage and denigrate Puerto Ricans, to make themselves feel better.

Everyone, in effect, looks for a lower level with respect to which they can appear proud and dominant. Racism provides all an expedient solution. One has simply to find someone lower than oneself, someone slightly more downtrodden, to discover an adequate target upon whom to heap one's contempt and scorn. *Racism offers satisfaction to one and all.*

8. Is a person's need for reassurance and self-affirmation really so dire that it must be obtained at the price of dehumanizing someone else? Does self-justification really rely on denigrating others? Once one apprehends the extent of it, the frequency with which it is adopted as a solution, one can only answer yes.

It is a fallacious and depraved solution, however, a mean-spirited and vain compensation above all; it falsifies all social standards and perspectives, and betrays all through itself by destroying the dignity of some in order to console the illusory dignity for others. But it must be admitted that it is *a form of solution for real problems,* a tranquilizer in the face of undeniable afflictions, and so widespread that it is surprising to find it absent anywhere.

It is a fact that the sick are comforted by the thought that others are in worse shape than themselves. They can be consoled by the dark thought that a few more steps yet exist between themselves and death, that they have not yet hit bottom if there are others who have fallen even further. "Look down below yourself" is the banal but accepted advice of popular wisdom. It is true that misery comforts itself by looking at misery. Is it so astonishing then that the racist finds repose from his misery by looking at that of others? Better, racism allows one to go one step further and impose hardship and adversity on the other, impart more misery than the other would ordinarily suffer, in order to find it there for his own consolation.

9. The existence of the other is never a matter of indifference. The fact of dread, or the terrible anxieties that can arise in the face of otherness, is a central component of racism and cannot be overemphasized. The stranger is always strange and frightening in some way—even someone who is just of another social class. And it is just a few steps from dread to hostility, and from hostility to violence. To relate positively to another, one must relax, and forget oneself; in effect, one needs to abandon oneself to the other to an extent, and identify with him or her. The stranger will not be acquitted until one succeeds in adopting him or her. Without that, the outsider's opacity and recalcitrant autonomy remain irksome, disturbing. How is one not to bear a grudge against foreigners who oblige one to remain on one's guard? Who require one to be armed against them? And the final step in all this inverted logic: these people whom we mistrust, whom we don't like, and whom we suspect and condemn in advance, how could they not want to do the same to us?

10. From that moment on, the cycle of passions will spin with its own momentum. These people, who probably detest us, surely therefore merit our hate. And must we not provide in advance for their possible aggressions, and attack them if need be? Many conflicts, at the individual and the group levels, are born and nourished largely on this mental sludge. Thus, the prime necessity lies in overcoming the fear

of the other and in calming the spirit afflicted by these contorted antipathies.

Ultimately, *the feeling of guilt is one of the most powerful engines of the racist operation.* Racism presents itself as one of the primary means of combating all forms of remorse. That is why both *privilege and oppression make such heavy use of it.* If oppression exists, someone has to be blamed for it; and if the oppressor will not own up to that himself, which would be intolerable, then the blame must fall on the oppressed. In short, *racism is a form of charging the oppressed for the crimes, whether actual or potential, of the oppressor.*[10]

Racism not only produces aggression, it is one of the manifestations of aggression, and aggression seems to be a very common mode of conduct for our species. It is always immediately available, ready at hand at a bargain price that can be charged to its victim. Why is this so? If the response appears banal, it should not be dismissed for precisely that reason. Humans are animals. And like most animals, when they are afraid, they attack or flee. When people feel fear, it is in the face of a perceived danger, whether real or imaginary, that is, in the face of the real or imaginary hostility of the other.

I will not address other fears here, such as fear of other animals, fear of physical catastrophe, or the metaphysical fear of the unknown. And yet, the fear of other animals does unleash similar reactions, which might explain "Man's" tendency to exterminate certain animals beyond the call of pragmatic necessity. And it is always possible for imaginary fears to blossom into myth, which then reflects back on human relations as a whole—suggesting the importance of myth in the human universe.[11] While xenophobia seems to concretize certain mythic anxieties, there are bestiaries that do the same for animal anxieties. Perhaps an iconographic map relating outsiders and animals would be instructive. But within the bounds of our present investigation, it is more important to recognize that humans are intraconflictual, and that fact sums up the human tragedy. The aggressiveness of each person or group responds to the aggressiveness of others, mediated by reciprocal fear.

How are we to evaluate this aggressiveness? Is it acquired or innate? The opinions of experts differ greatly on the question. But what importance does that really have right now if it remains something that must be taken into account on a daily basis? We hope that the future will take care of itself, but the past has certainly testified more than eloquently to the fact that "man" is a predator to the detriment of nature, of other species, and of his own kind (see note 3 in "Description"). He covets and takes the things he needs, even from those close to him. Aggressive toward others, he continually kindles their fear and aggressiveness toward him in turn, which then keeps his own burning. An endless circle: one aggressive stance nourishes another. It is like an old habit, but at the "species level" and somehow linked to survival. Permanently menacing and permanently menaced, every person has been, up to the present, surrounded by perils that she or he instigates or that are instigated by the other. Besieged by enemies, one owes one's health only to strong responses, both offensive and defensive.

Up to now, this system has functioned fairly well—too well, in fact. Despite vast technological and moral progress, it cannot be seriously said that things have changed much in this regard. The unmitigated cruelty to be found in the historical record, even the most recent, is horrifying. We continue to confine and to decimate entire animal species for our food, clothing, and warmth, or because we think they are obnoxious (that is to say, out of fear); even worse, we do it for our mere entertainment. It is said that this is the price of our survival, that every living species does as much. Maybe, but not with such systematic ruthlessness. We have become so accustomed to it that we no longer reflect on the meaning of a hunting trophy, or a bullfight, or a simple fishing party, or even the circus. The processes of training, and the vast business of killing, for the purposes of profit or pleasure, all form part of a war on animals. Yet beyond that, the human is the only species who has invented, for its own kind, the prison, prison camps, torture, genocide . . . and racism. In the words of Freud, a broken old man on the eve of the Second World War, presaging its horrors: "Man is a filthy beast."

Every living thing, animal or vegetable, will search for what favors its survival, and will defend itself against what puts it in danger; in this ongoing war, there is a need for both defense and offense, a necessity to steal and to kill, to aggress and to repel aggression. But "man" is the only being who has set this whole process in motion against his own kind. And racism is one of the cogs in that infernal machine. That is, "man" is the only animal who, in order to justify himself, despises, humiliates, and systematically annihilates other people, in body and in mind. Furthermore, the discursive dimension that is highlighted by every act of self-justification is not beside the point. Humans are beings of language, which means that they repeat, announce, punctuate, and memorialize all experience in images and in words. It is a useful augmentation; it permits the preservation of gestures, elaboration, and interpretation of present experiences for the future. And for racism, this same discursive level constitutes *a permanent laboratory in which to prepare the destruction (social, psychological, or physical) of the other who has already been named the adversary.* "Man" knows—or rather, he has learned in the course of his long history—that while he must struggle against his own kind, he must also live with them. In other words, he must, to a certain extent, be at home with them. He aggresses, but he explains; he is an aggressor who argues, and an arguer who makes excuses for himself.

Thus, *racism is always both a discourse and an action*; it is a discourse that prepares an action, and an action that legitimates itself through a discourse. Ancient warriors in combat used to insult their adversaries, denouncing their real or assumed inferiorities, their "defective children" and their "tainted ancestors," all the way back to tutelary gods, in order to render the adversary despicable enough to deserve defeat and death. But the insults turned against themselves. If the enemy were so weak and corrupt, how dangerous could he be? In reality, one insults the enemy in order to explain one's attack in the first place, as much as to diminish him as an enemy. It is undoubtedly theater. Racism is also theater, a querulous polemic that makes everything about the other something it is not, whether physique, customs, history, culture, religion. But it gets out of hand and becomes too shrill; in straining his voice, the racializing speaker becomes suspect of not really believing it all. Racism is an emotional and rhetorical incantation whose purpose is to proclaim one's own power and to exorcise one's fear of adversity. Against the unknown, everything must be brought into play, and the stranger presents the most formidable figure of the unknown.

Can this infernal machine be derailed? We had better admit that it will not be easy. The human world is dangerous for humans. Each person, and each group, represents a potential threat. Given "Man" as we know "him," in our present social environment, this latent violence must be taken into account. Up to now, a truly humane order, free from reciprocal threats, has seemed utopian. Indeed, the inverse is the rule: those who deploy racism seem the best adapted, the most natural. It is important for both minority and majority not to appear to be weak, not to be disarmed. It is to strengthen oneself that the foreigner is made a sacrificial offering to the spirit of hostility.

What might offer a resolution to this tragic intrahuman confrontation, to this war of all against all? *Racism is a form of war.* And there we glimpse its real face behind all of its shadowy disguises. Up to now, we have disregarded the innateness of aggressivity. We can no longer afford to do that if we wish to look to the future. If aggressiveness is not an inherent psychic drive, then there may be hope for better human relations. Yet even if it is innate, humans are nevertheless products of both their nature and their conditions of existence, so a transformation of those conditions could be beneficial—on the assumption, of course, that there is the ability and the will.

It turns out that there is actually a lot to work with. The idea of moral behavior is not an entirely utopian one; like violence itself, its roots lie in the individual and collective human personality. In each person, with respect to others, there is both attraction and repulsion, dependence and supremacy (see *Dependence*). Though Christian anti-Semitism certainly exists, many Jews were saved by Christians during the war, some of whom paid for their generosity with their lives. Moslems did the same thing, even in the midst of occupied Paris; many refugees lived hidden in the basement of the mosque. The bourgeois Jews of New York were among the prime defenders of Black Americans, who actually didn't like them very much.

However profuse or infrequent such actions may be, they are encouraging for the future; each person is both a danger to other people and a salvation. The contradiction is only apparent; each must act to assure his or her own survival, but survival is always linked to that of others as a matter of necessity and opportunity. The same obscure urgency that has thrown humanity against itself since the origin of the species also suggests the basis of a contract. If each man is often a wolf toward other men, he is also a father, a son, a brother, a brother-in-law, and a cousin of men, whom he insists on saving, sometimes at the risk of his own life. A man is the male toward all human females, and a woman is the female toward all males—even if there is at times violent conflict to take a certain woman or man away from others. Adult humans are the fathers and mothers of all young men and women because, beyond the individual level, the species can be preserved only through its offspring. At the appearance of danger, all adults find themselves spontaneously in agreement: the children come first.

It occurred to me to write that racism is natural and anti-racism is acquired. That would have been half-wrong; they both have their roots in us. The obsessiveness of racism exists, but there also exist inclinations that carry us toward others, both to seek or to offer solace. We know, by intuition and by experience, that these inclinations are innate, from our first breath to our last, by virtue of our real reciprocal dependence. Indeed, these two contradictory manifestations of our being have a more profound unity whose source lies in that prior spirit that drives all life to persevere and to survive, by whatever means, whether antagonistic or not. They are two solutions to the same problem of survival.

. . . And Some practical lessons

In light of all this, what are some of the practical lessons that can be drawn?

1. First and foremost, *we must be conscious of racism,* not just in others but in ourselves, individually and collectively. To denounce it in others is easy, convenient, and, we might add, contradictory; it is to demand that the other abandon his or her aggressive hostilities without renouncing our own. To disarm the racism in ourselves first, in order to combat it in our own conduct, is the best way to obtain its eventual remission in others. That is the first step, the price to be paid in advance.

Though each person needs to develop his or her own modes of vigilance, there is one that has served me well as a rule of thumb. It is to conceptualize all instances of human difference that have been given social importance through a form of *double-entry bookkeeping.* A Parisian worker once complained, in an official hearing, about the smell of Caribbean sausage that frequently invaded the stairwells of his building. The investigator, with a certain churlishness, asked him what his reaction would be if the odor had been of cabbage. The man brightened and exclaimed, "I love that smell—it is that of my childhood." He has, of course, the right to love the smell of cabbage and to continue to prefer it to that of Caribbean sausage. But if he told himself that to his Caribbean neighbor the odor of sausage was perhaps delicious and that of cabbage detestable, he might be more indulgent. He would no longer be able to draw metaphysical conclusions about the singular and repulsive "nature" of people from the Antilles or, above all, prejudge them in order to justify active hostility. Maybe he would arrive at no longer taking himself as the criteriological standard by which to judge others as abnormal or substandard, which constitutes the core of racist practice. As Diderot said, "What right do you have over him that he has not over you?"[12]

What is needed is an exercise of empathy, which means training ourselves in the difficult task of *participating in the other.* It is, of course, an old proverbial thought: to understand the suffering of the other, his humiliation, his pain at being insulted or struck, one has to put oneself in his place—in thought, at least, through a kind of creative conceptual overlap. Or, to go a step further, one could try living some of the same situations. "To live in the skin of a Black person" is the project the White American author John Howard Griffith set for himself in what turned out to be a truly extraordinary experience.[13] Similarly, many political militants have set out to share the daily existence of the average industrial or agricultural worker, as have the worker-priests. In that way, the imagination, so often lazy when it comes to others, can be dragged into connection with others by its own body and mind. In effect, anti-racism should be first of all a form of mental hygiene, an adoption of a relativist view that would be more tolerant of others and of their cultural institutions.

Not that racism is an illness, as some people

think. Such a concept is only another expediency; it implies that racism is a rare occurrence that, in affecting certain individuals, highlights a personality problem. It has been suggested that certain personality types are predisposed to racism. Maybe. But in saying that, one also disguises a hidden fear behind a problematic scientific notion. The thought that racism only affects certain perverse kinds of people would of course be somewhat reassuring; they would just have to be cured to see the sickness disappear. But unfortunately, I don't think that will work! Racism is not an illness but an archaic attitude common to the species. No psychotherapy administered to self-declared racists, assuming they consented, would eliminate it. What is necessary, instead, is constant and general circumspection, both individual and collective efforts that call on psychology, sociology, and politics all at once.

2. The struggle against racism requires a continual pedagogy, from infancy to death. Each child, which is the promise of a full person, carries within the seeds of fear and of violence. Sometimes this will express itself in the torture or even "involuntary" killing of an animal or of another child. Such "accidents" are well known: a pencil "inadvertently" driven into the eye of a baby brother, a bullet fired while "playing" with the family pistol. But in children, there is also a need to feel cared for, to be given confidence and identification; there is a need for a certain devotion, an attention that must be given to the young, as well as a need to return their own admiring attachment to older people. Let us just say that these

positive sentiments are continually threatened by negative ones, by the inevitable incidents of family life or of school and society. The arrival of a new baby, for instance, produces jealousy, perhaps, or a fear of going without, an insecurity and uncertainty with regard to the parents, a rivalry among companions, or various terrors and inclinations to destroy, to injure others as well as oneself. The tasks of education are vast. If the possibility of killing is present to each person from the moment of birth, one must carefully tame and socialize all dangerous and idiotic desires—and, equally, strengthen healthy ones. In particular, it means to teach children, young people, and adults not only not to fear differences, but to enjoy them; that is, to cherish and embrace others *[aimer]*. To really like someone does not mean simply to seek one's own image in them—that would be to love oneself through them—but to like in them what only belongs to them, that is, precisely the ways in which they differ. It is necessary to encourage and cultivate this approach to people, as a sense of friendship and love.

None of this is obvious. Under the aegis of difference people are oppressed, robbed, and killed, war against other nations is rationalized, and minority groups are persecuted. It is sufficient to stigmatize another as a heretic or dissident. For those stigmatized, the process of devaluing differences can sometimes initiate an inverse process that reifies aspects of their own tradition that are suffocating or even onerous. One sees this dialectic at work among immigrant groups. In response, one might conclude, a bit prematurely, that one must struggle boldly against all difference. However, that is not really an option if we do not wish to resign ourselves to permanent social war. Instead, we must teach, encourage, and favor friendship and feelings of solidarity. This won't be easy, especially when our educational systems sadly provide little space for human sentiment. This deficiency is symptomatic. Excessive trust runs the risk of disarming one in the face of one's companions or associates. We are familiar with the stifled giggles or sneers that greet an adolescent, a dreamer, or an artist who calls for more loyal or generous behavior, or the sad astonishment of young people when they discover that social reality is very different from the morality they had been taught. To guard against these weaknesses, we must bring ourselves together. As with military disarmament, a unilateral measure risks being very costly. In a word, if it is fraternity we seek to extend to the entire species, it will have to be affirmed by all the world's teachers and advocated by people of all ages. It is the discernment, exorcism, and diversion of real murderous impulses that we are talking about, and it will require that all the appropriate techniques of teaching be unceasingly put in effect. That is, we must do everything so that people stop arming themselves against each other. All programs of education should include the denunciation of aggression and, correlatively, the teaching of solidarity. If the practice of preventive medicine is a good idea, then why not prevention of disorders of the spirit? Of course, there are conflicts in which the stakes are very real, but there are also conflicts that start only because each side believes itself threatened by the other. Many people dislike their neighbors because they believe themselves disliked by them. Since the apprehension of real or imagined evil is one of the ingredients of aggressiveness, *anything that diminishes fear will have a beneficial effect*. The mastery of old emotions and the correct evaluation of danger are surely more salutary than brutal impulsive reactions.

3. The core of all teaching is an individual relation to the student, even when the teaching occurs in large groups. But *teaching must also address itself to the social, to the collective,* and that is the role of politics. Politics is a collective form of behavior in the name of certain values and in view of a greater efficacy. Racism is always dangerous to its prey, but it is also injurious to the racist group because it boomerangs. Hate feeds hate. Like all aggression, racism deforms the face and the conduct of the racist himself—just as colonialism transformed the Europeans, even those of good will, into colonialists. A great degree of lucidity is required to discern the criminal effects on oneself of fear or authority or privilege. An intelligent politics would at least try to channel these effects and to lessen their frequency and intensity, if not eliminate them altogether. How? On two levels, I would think: that of opinion and that of conduct.

Opinion contributes to hostility in the sense that it precedes it as motive or follows it as justification. Anti-racism proposes the suppression of all manifestations of racism, in speech and act. I admit to having agreed with this idea. When the Second

World War ended and we emerged from its horrors, though fascism had been defeated on the battlefield, it had not totally lost the battle of ideas. Its ideology had still to be uprooted in order to prevent its political return. The freedom to express injurious opinion did not seem to be worth defending. Today, I recognize that the problem is more complicated, above all for a democracy. To outlaw an opinion, however unjust, is again the commission of an injustice. The risk is always of swinging from Charybdis to Scylla.

What should be done then? Today, I would say, *to opinion one must oppose opinion.* Naturally, the social body must provide itself with the educational and informational means (the school curricula and the media) to counter opinions judged dangerous to the group and the subgroups that constitute it. If racism were confined to the level of opinion, so much the better, but when it becomes a real racism, that is, if opinion reveals itself to be the prelude to open hostility, then it must be dealt with by other means.

Of course, it is not always easy to distinguish between a pure opinion and a program for action. This invokes the problem of incitement, which surpasses the attempt to persuade. The appeal to violence is the embryo of an enactment of violence. Nevertheless, on the whole, *it is the actual passage to action that must remain the criterion for political counteraction.* Between the two poles of opinion and action, opinion should be tolerated but aggressiveness firmly prohibited. One cannot force people to like each other, but one can stop them from attacking.[14]

For liberal thinkers, the idea of active repression, whether political or judicial or otherwise, is a problem. It suggests that one has adopted the enemy's methods. But when racist opinion transforms itself into active practice, it behooves one to stop it by other than merely discursive means. Otherwise, one becomes stuck in what I call "sentimental anti-racism."[15] Let me say a word about that. For me, an emotional or sentimental anti-racism is guilty of both an insufficiency of analysis and a timidity—and I have often said as much, at times with some irony. The liberals' generosity blinds them, for example, to the extent of the phenomenon, to the often murderous violence of racism on the one hand and to its ability to take hold of its victims and turn them against those who are even weaker on the other. For instance, statistically, mixed marriages are more difficult than others, but instead of denying it, it would be much more valuable to engender in our young people a sober understanding of this, and prepare them to outmaneuver and defeat its problems in their own ways. As always, a deep awareness of a situation is the necessary condition for appropriate action within it. I have already discussed this with respect to both the colonized and the Jews.

This two-sided critique of sentimental anti-racism has ironically been an invitation to some who, by rhetorical adeptness, political opportunism, or aberrant reasoning, have sought to paint anti-racism with the same brush as racism itself—even to the point of repeating, in self-defense, the polemics of the so-called new right.[16] One would not really want to lump together those who fool themselves through indulgence and those who really advocate a doctrine of exclusion. But the naïveté of some sentimental anti-racists can be annoying—in their complaisance, for instance, toward certain abusive excesses. I have been told of certain Third World students who accuse other female students of racism for not going to bed with them, which is obviously over the line. In general, one should guard against making an accusation of racism too easily; it is a disservice to the struggle. Neither should one confuse racism with the politics of immigration, which sometimes happens, even though the former may have had an influence on the latter. Some politicians have used anti-racism as an electoral argument; but, of course, that is less serious than using racism to the same end. None of this is commensurable with actual racism, which does real damage to human relations. But we must not fool ourselves about our target. Or, let it be done on purpose, with a clear understanding of tactical goals. Here, too, the distinction between racism and heterophobia would be of service.

The important point is what our common philosophy should be. Here is what I think is essential.

The struggle against racism coincides, at least in part, with the struggle against all oppression. There will always be the necessity for struggle. Racism is a perverted sentiment that is the result, the expression, and the matrix of real situations that must be changed if it is to be brought to an end. In order for racism to disappear, it will be necessary that *the oppressed cease to be the oppressed,* that is, recognized as the convenient victim, as the incarnation of an image the oppressor had invented. But it will also be necessary that *the oppressor cease to be an oppressor,* cease to require that others be under his thumb, cease to have need for that, and thus cease to need justification for it.

It is not a question, of course, of neutralizing all aggressiveness, as some racists ironically imply while proposing a sort of offhand philosophical virility, which, in reality, rests upon a contempt for people. A certain aggressiveness is important. It is necessary that one be able to feel antipathy and strike back; it would be dangerous and unwholesome if one were not able to do that.

Moments of uncertainty when faced with others are normal, but this should not become a weapon or an alibi for injustice. The racist denigration of others must not be allowed to extend itself to permission to assault or oppress those others, nor must it be allowed to transform itself into a mythology about them. One's anxiety must not become permission to bully a person because that person may belong to a certain group, even one not in good repute.

It will not be necessary to deny the real differences between people, as many anti-racists desire, driven by their simplistic humanism. On the contrary, *differences must be lucidly recognized,* embraced and respected as such. Others must be granted their being as other, with all the enrichment of life that might be possible through their very differences. The recognition of the other, with his or her differences, does not prevent dialogue; on the contrary, it not only calls for dialogue but is the necessary condition for it. To deny difference, to close one's eyes to that indubitable aspect of human reality, risks setting the stage for future upheaval; it sets the stage for that day when sudden changes in social conditions impose the deployment of those same differences against those who had decided to so generously ignore them. Such was the experience of many teachers and humanists in the colonies.[17]

To refuse racism is to choose a certain conception of humanity; it means a reconciliation among different constituent groups, thus a relative unification, not of all in each other but of each in relation to others. Conversely, humanity cannot unify itself in this relative way except through intergroup equality, and equality between the individuals who compose each group. Ordinarily, this is what would be called *universalism.*

Two principal objections have been made to universalism. The first is that it is ineffective and even hypocritical as a philosophy. The second, which flows from the first, is that it is obsolete, like an old horse put out to pasture not for having been used up but for having demonstrated its inherent and tragic uselessness. The Jewish universalism of its prophets, the Christian universalism of its churches, the Islamic universalism of its indulgent community of believers, of people of the Book, the Marxist universalism of proletarian unity through which the eventual well-being of all by means of the Revolution is projected have none of them succeeded in putting an end to violence, to injustice, or to massacre. At best, up to now, universalism has remained a utopia. Or worse, it has served as an alibi for distracting attention from existent and always recurring privilege. For the dominated, universalism has always been a false philosophy that has served to cover their real oppression with a cloak of abstract virtue. This was true in the slave trade, the industrialization of Europe, and the building of colonial empires. To claim that men are brothers while holding some of them in slavery is to be complicit in the crime.

Is a universalism possible that would not be either a trap or a utopia?

Paradoxically, instead of renouncing it, what is needed is more universalism, that is, the passage from an abstract to a concrete universalism. *It is not sufficient simply to condemn racism; it is necessary to act on the collective social conditions of its existence.* In effect, universalism must pass from being just a philosophy to becoming an activity. A double activity, actually, both negative and positive: a struggle against oppression and a struggle for effective and reciprocal fraternity.

In the last analysis, because racism is a direct or indirect manifestation of dominance, it becomes possible only if one has the means to dominate another under the guise of an opinion. The practical implication is that *to push back racism, one must combat all forms of domination.* We can actually see the truth of this unfolding at the present time, practically as if under laboratory conditions. The case of the Arabs is one such instance. Insofar as they had been colonized, there exists an Arabophobia. It has begun to recede because the Arab nations are becoming more powerful economically. Yet, at the same time, immigrant Arab workers in Europe continue to suffer from it, since their relation to the structure that had dominated them has not changed. Judeophobia offers another picture of such reciprocal effects; it varies directly with the vicissitudes of Israel, perceived as the nation of the Jews. There is an attenuation of Judeophobia at those moments when that state is ascendant (e.g., in the realization of its pioneering efforts, in war victories, in succeeding at its enterprises), and it reappears when Israel loses ground. The attitude of the possessing classes toward workers in Europe has changed significantly with the construction and recognition of the unions.

Universality ultimately must imply real reciprocity, or it is a fraud. The truth is, universalism is a wish, not a fact; a value, not an incontestable reality. Human society is not unified, but it moves toward unification, to which universalism can contribute.

In the end, I ask that one reflect on this. When is it that robbery or murder are considered crimes? When they are part of an inclusive communal law.[18] If one moves beyond geographic or juridical boundaries, traditional scruples tend to fall away. Invading soldiers rape women and take people's belongings with impunity, which they then call spoils. The foreigner is the one who, not having been raised under our laws, is not protected by them. That is, the foreigner does not belong to the same community as we do. Among different groups, violence continues because these groups have not yet drawn up a mutually inclusive law; that is, they have not yet founded a common community. Inversely, each time that a community, whether interethnic or international, is affirmed, injustice and war decline. In the United States, the North and the South brought their war to a halt through reunification, but Black people continue an internal war because they are not seen as integrated in the American nation. War should no longer have existed among the Soviet republics, but problems arose because, from time to time, one partner or another felt itself disfavored by the law of union. In short, the more people consider and treat each other under the same rubric, the more violence declines; the more they consider and treat others through otherness, the greater the risk of xenophobia, that is, of violence.[19]

The latest events in Poland provide a bitter illustration of this question.[20] Why such intense emotion throughout Europe? Legitimate, to be sure, but excessive compared to other tragedies that strike the rest of the world. Two hundred dead was a scandal in Poland, but some forty thousand children die of starvation every day in the countries of the Third World. Two million children, throughout the world, are delivered into prostitution. Why is there a difference in the reaction of Europeans if not that they regard Poland as part of themselves and the Third World as an alien universe?

Evidently, I am a moderate optimist. The struggle against racism will be long and probably never totally successful. Humans *[l'homme]* being what they are, one cannot for the moment hope for a total end to racist behavior. Even mixed marriage is not a remedy; the example of Brazil is hardly encouraging. There, rather than disappear, racism has created a more complex color hierarchy. In the Caribbean, social classes correspond to a scale of colors. It is as if racism can always find, in each case, the tactic or machination that will work.[21]

But yet, humans being what they are, the job can and should be undertaken. People are both angels and beasts; the angel must be assisted in prevailing over the beast. Or, more prosaically, reciprocal dependence must be strengthened as the foundation of the social bond. Whatever the importance of a conflict between individuals or groups, the relative stability of social structures confirms a reciprocal need to engender an inclusive common law of life. Racism represents precisely the inverse process, since it is a temptation to exclude and the legitimation of exclusion.

The pessimist will object that this is pure rhetoric designed to repackage the same old conduct. But even rhetorical effort is not wasted. Beyond its perversity, the racist discourse is a defense mechanism *[plaidoyer]* and an alibi. But every search for an alibi also contains within it an implicit recognition of the law. Racism is a structure of aggression that claims, and is given, a presupposed rationality. This pretense is the sign of its cunning and its false assertion of its own humanity. That is why no one wishes to own up to being racist; no one wishes to consent, in their heart, to renounce all humanity. The most hardened racists at least have one ear that hears, a port directly connected to that part of themselves that does not totally approve of iniquity and oppression. The mania and the horror of Nazism comes from what it had renounced of all legitimization, that it had made racism a philosophy if not a total conception of humanity.

Is that all there is? The infinite task before us can be discouraging in that it must always be begun again. Up to now, all peace has only been a truce between two wars, yet still we hope and long for peace. Health is fragile, and death is always in the offing, yet still we struggle to keep ourselves in good health. *The struggle against racism is the condition of our collective social health.* It encompasses the fundamental moral discussions of love or hate of the other, of justice or injustice, equality or oppression, or, in a word, one's very humanity. The essence of morality is respect for the other. Our honor as humans will be to construct a more human world. In the meanwhile, so that even animals may some day find a world of peace and security, let us act so that no one is any longer treated like a beast.

In short, faced with otherness and the real problems it poses, there are two possible approaches: war and dialogue. The temptation to vanquish the other, to reduce him or her to servitude, and to give oneself an ideological pretext for doing so, racist or otherwise, is certainly quite common and, it would seem, more profitable than the initiation of dialogue or of a just reciprocity.

The intervening ethical and political option, which we have left aside during this investigation, can now no longer be ignored. The choice that presents itself is between an attitude and conduct that crushes and humiliates certain people for the benefit of others, and an attitude and conduct that accords from the beginning an equal dignity to all. This is where the line between racists and anti-racists is drawn. Racism accepts the norm of primitive violence and pretends to justify it, which leads to a certain philosophy of Man and of human relations. Anti-racism refuses this rift between people, with its definitive classifications into inferior and superior. It prioritizes dialogue and agrees to put in question all situations of acquisition, dominance, and privilege. *It is a definitive question of two visions of humanity and two philosophies.*

One last word: we cannot hide from the difficulty of the struggle against racism.

It is not easy to put oneself in the place of the oppressed, whatever that might be. And a sympathetic identification with the other becomes even more difficult when the oppression is more severe; that is, when the social and psychological distance between oneself and other people is large. The chasm between the colonized and the colonialists, for instance, was often so large that even White Europeans of good will could not imagine what was happening in the souls of their native domestic servants ("they are impenetrable"). For the oppressed, there exists a sense of despair and of futility that conditions and tempers every feeling and mood, and which does not exist for the non-oppressed. The non-oppressed can, by definition, remove themselves from any situation. As heartwarming as the undertakings of the American writer Griffith were, in staining himself dark and living among the Black people of the South, he knew that he could, whenever he so desired, return to the North, reannounce his whiteness to the world, and put an end to his voluntary nightmare. One could never completely put oneself in the place of the Black person, or in that of a Jew who has lost family to the crematoria.

In that sense, the teaching in the schools has to overcome the teachings of the street—and of the family milieu. Indeed, it has to defeat an entire cultural tradition, one that only becomes more tenacious the more ambiguous or incoherent it gets. The transformation of the objective conditions of existence that alone might permit an end to oppression is not going to happen tomorrow. And it does not depend only on the efforts of anti-racists. Nothing guarantees, besides, that a new political order, for which many may yet struggle hard, will not deploy in turn a racist alibi, a proven resource at times of social crisis, for its own purposes.

The struggle against racism will be long, difficult, without intermission, without remission, probably never achieved.

Yet, for this very reason, it is a struggle to be undertaken without surcease and without concessions. One cannot be indulgent toward racism; one must not even let the monster in the house, especially not in a mask. To give it merely a foothold means to augment the bestial part in us and in other people, which is to diminish what is human. *To accept the racist universe to the slightest degree is to endorse fear, injustice, and violence.* It is to accept the persistence of the dark history in which we still largely live. It is to agree that the outsider will always be a possible victim (and which man is not himself an outsider relative to someone else?). Racism illustrates, in sum, the inevitable negativity of the condition of the dominated; that is, it illuminates in a certain sense the entire human condition. The anti-racist struggle, difficult though it is, and always in question, is nevertheless one of the prologues to the ultimate passage from animality to humanity. *In that sense, we cannot fail to rise to the racist challenge.*

However, it remains true that one's moral conduct only emerges from a choice; one has to want it. It is a choice among other choices, and always debatable in its foundations and its consequences. Let us say, broadly speaking, that the choice to conduct oneself morally is the condition for the establishment of a human order, for which racism is the very negation. This is almost a redundancy. One cannot found a moral order, let alone a legislative order, on racism, because racism signifies the exclusion of the other, and his or her subjection to violence and domination. From an ethical point of view, if one can deploy a little religious language, racism is "the truly capital sin."[22] It is not an accident that almost all of humanity's spiritual traditions counsel respect for the weak, for orphans, widows, or strangers. It is not just a question of theoretical morality and disinterested commandments. Such unanimity in the safeguarding of the other suggests the real utility of such sentiments. All things considered, we have an interest in banishing injustice, because injustice engenders violence and death.

Of course, this is debatable. There are those who think that if one is strong enough, the assault on and oppression of others is permissible. But no one is ever sure of remaining the strongest. One day, perhaps, the roles will be reversed. All unjust society contains within itself the seeds of its own death. It is probably smarter to treat others with respect so that they treat you with respect. "Recall," says the Bible, "that you were once a stranger in Egypt," which means both that you ought to respect the stranger because you were a stranger yourself and that you risk becoming one again someday. It is an ethical and a practical appeal—indeed, it is a contract, however implicit it might be. In short, *the refusal of racism is the condition for all theoretical and practical morality.* Because, in the end, the ethical choice commands the political choice, a just society must be a society accepted by all. If this contractual principle is not accepted, then only conflict, violence, and destruction will be our lot. If it is accepted, we can hope someday to live in peace. True, it is a wager, but the stakes are irresistible.

APPENDIXES

APPENDIX A
AN ATTEMPT AT A DEFINITION

Translated by Eleanor Levieux
Reprinted from Albert Memmi, Dominated Man *(New York: Orion Press, 1968), 185–95.*
Originally published in Le Nef *19–20 (Paris, 1964)*

Of course, the definition that follows is the result of all the following commentary and analysis. I am beginning with it for memory's sake, in an expository procedure like that used by mathematicians. These pages could just as well be read in reverse order: sections III, II, and I. The best way would be to run rapidly through the definition and the analysis even if it is necessary to come back to them in light of the commentary.

I. DEFINITION

Racism is the generalized and final assigning of values to real or imaginary differences, to the accuser's benefit and at his victim's expense, in order to justify the former's own privileges or aggression.

II. ANALYSIS OF THE RACIST ATTITUDE

This analysis reveals four essential elements:

1. Stressing the real or imaginary differences between the racist and his victim.
2. Assigning values to these differences, to the advantage of the racist and the detriment of his victim.
3. Trying to make them absolutes by generalizing from them and claiming that they are final.
4. Justifying any present or possible aggression or privilege.[1]

III. COMMENTARY

The term *racism* is obviously not adequate to cover a mechanism so widespread. It is too narrow, just as *anti-Semitism* is, on the contrary, too broad. Strictly speaking, it would apply to a theory of *biological differences*. The Nazis, adding to the ideas of the apologists for the slave trade and for colonization, included a system for establishing a political, moral, and cultural hierarchy of human groups according to their biological differences.

A Widespread Mechanism

The racist actually bases his accusation on a biological or a cultural difference, from which he generalizes to cover the whole of the defendant's personality, his life, and the group to which he belongs. Sometimes the biological trait is unclear or even missing. We can see that the mechanism is infinitely more varied, more complex, and—unhappily—more common than the term *racism* would imply. It ought to be replaced by another term or other words showing what varied and at the same time what interrelated forms racism can take. (Perhaps by a pair of terms: *aggression-justification,* for instance, which sums up quite well the general mechanism we are about to describe.)

Stressing the Difference

The first form of racism consists of stressing a difference between the accuser and his victim. But revealing a characteristic differentiating two individuals or two groups does not in itself constitute a racist attitude. After all, this is part of what any student of the human sciences does. The assertion that there is a difference takes on a special significance in the racist context: by emphasizing the difference, the racist aims to intensify or cause the exclusion, the separation by which the victim is placed outside the community or even outside humanity.

The colonizer discriminates to demonstrate the impossibility of including the colonized in the community: because he would be too biologically or culturally different, technically or politically inept, etc. Anti-Semitism attempts, by depicting the Jew as radically foreign and strange, to explain the isolation of the Jew, the quarantine under which he is placed. Making use of the difference is an essential step in the racist process, but it is not the difference that always entails racism: it is racism that makes use of the difference.

The Difference Is Real or Imaginary

If the difference is missing, the racist invents one; if the difference exists, he interprets it to his own advantage. He emphasizes only those differences that contribute to his argument. In other words, the difference is real or imaginary, important or slight in itself.

One important point, however: contrary to the view commonly held by the sentimental anti-racist, I do not think that the difference singled out by the racist is always the work of imagination, sheer madness, or a malevolent lie. The racist can base his argument on a real trait, whether biological, psychological, cultural, or social—such as the color of the Black man's skin or the solid tradition of the Jew.[2]

Of course, the racist can make up a difference, if he needs one to construct his argument, but his method is not confined to imagining more or less fantastic differential traits or to the mere observation of sometimes genuine differences. It always adds an interpretation of such differences, a prejudiced attempt to place a value on them.[3] To put it briefly, the difference is assigned a value in such a way as to discredit the defendant and reflect credit on his accuser.

Placing a Value on the Difference

Here is certainly one of the key elements in the racist process. Explicitly or implicitly, the assigning of values is intended to prove two things: the inferiority of the victim and the superiority of the racist. Better still, it proves the one by the other: inferiority of the Black race automatically means superiority of the White. Inferiority of the colonized vividly demonstrates the superiority of the colonizer. Thus, the assigning of values is negative and positive at the same time: negative value of the victim, therefore positive value of the accuser. It follows that:

1. Any difference separating the victim from his accuser is likely to be suspect and deserve denunciation. Racism begins by assigning a negative value and, simply by changing a minus to a plus sign, can turn any difference, whether real or imagined, into a positive quality on the part of the accuser. In the racist way of thinking, difference is evil. This means, of course, the difference characterizing the victim in relation to the accuser, who is taken as the point of reference. It is not Whiteness that differentiates the White man from the Black; it is Blackness that disastrously differentiates the Black man from the White.
2. The racist will do his utmost to stretch the distance between the minus and the plus signs, to maximize the difference. The smaller he makes his victim, the bigger he becomes; the more drastically he marks the difference at the

expense of his victim, the more drastically he turns it to his own advantage.[4]

That is why a simple biological or cultural difference, which is sometimes a real one, brings a whole crowd of meanings in its wake: the biology of the Jew becomes a repulsive biology, an unhealthful one. One step further, and it becomes heavy with a specific, harmful psychology, then with a metaphysical life of its own, etc. . . . We go from biology to ethics, from ethics to politics, from politics to metaphysics.

Once a value has been assigned, the coherence of the consequences emerges, and it is apparent that the noxious and inflammatory difference, overwhelming the victim and flattering his accuser, must be made absolute. If the accuser wants to be radically superior, then the difference must be made radical.

The Difference Is Generalized

So the discriminatory process enters the stage of generalization, "totalization." One thing leads to another until all of the victim's personality is characterized by the difference, and all of the members of his social group are targets for the accusation.

1. In this perspective it is easier to understand why biological racism is so successful; it fits in particularly well. The disastrous difference is echoed, as it were, in a substratum: it penetrates the flesh, the blood, and the genes of the victim. It is transformed into fate, destiny, heredity. From then on, the victim's very being is contaminated, and likewise every manifestation of

that being: behavior, body, and soul. Rarely does biological racism fail to give rise to psychological and cultural racism. In fact, the whole might be called an ethnism.

2. If the difference penetrates so profoundly into the being of the victim, it must also penetrate all his family, who are part of the same being. (See *The Colonizer and the Colonized,* "The Mark of the Plural.")

This is not actually a generalization: the relation between the individual trait and the collective trait is, so to speak, dialectic. Each of the defendant's real or supposed defects is extended to all his equals, but it is in the name of an implied collective defect that the defendant is condemned. From the greed of one Jew the anti-Semite concludes that all Jews are greedy and decides that no single Jew can be trusted because all Jews are greedy. The same is true with the stereotype of the lazy colonized.

Racism, on whatever level it occurs, always includes this collective element, which is, of course, one of the best ways of totalizing the situation: there must be no loophole by which any Jew, any colonized, or any Black man could escape this social determinism.

The Difference Is Final

It is easy to understand how the same movement also extends through time, back into the past and forward into the future. The Jew has always been greedy, the Black man has always been inferior.

Conclusion: the Jew will always be greedy, the Black man will always be inferior. There is no hope of a change, no salvation to be expected. Globalization, totalization, social generalization, and temporal generalization—all tend to a single purpose which, in the extreme, would be a substantiation of the difference, than of the victim as a figure. Thus, there is said to be a sort of absolute Black man, a kind of absolute Jew. They are negative figures, of course; definitively and absolutely negative. In the Middle Ages, as we know, the Jew finally became one of the incarnations of the devil, and in our own country he became the radical and antithetical enemy of the Nazis. In the same way the Black man has become one of the inferior categories of the human species. In the extreme, racism merges into myth.

At this point the whole structure takes leave of reality, from which it had derived its strength for a time, and follows its own coherence, moving from mere accusation to myth through the successive stages by which the victim is stripped of value. Broadly speaking, the process is one of gradual dehumanization. The racist ascribes to his victim a series of surprising traits, calling him incomprehensible, impenetrable, mysterious, strange, disturbing, and so on. Slowly he makes of his victim a sort of animal, a thing, or simply a symbol.

As the outcome of this effort to expel him from any human community, the victim is chained once and for all to his destiny of misfortune, derision, and guilt. And as a counterpart, the accuser is assured once and for all of keeping his role as rightful judge.

Justification of the Accuser

While racism moves toward myth, the myth refers back to the racist.

It is in the racist himself that the motives for racism lie. A superficial analysis is enough to reveal them, whether in individual or collective aggression.

I will not repeat the now-classic analyses of two phenomena: the scapegoat and the foreigner corrupting the national soul. We are already familiar with the way a group of human beings, in order to rid itself of certain guilt feelings, projects them onto an object, an animal, a man, or another group, which it accuses and punishes in its own stead. Nor will I linger over the alibi type of racism, an excuse for individual aggression. Competition on the economic front, rivalry between intellectuals or artists—these can give rise to racism, as a way of justifying a priori every difficulty the accuser runs into and his behavior toward his adversary. There is even a less sordid, distinctly individual motivation[5] that has been largely overlooked so far. A certain embarrassment when faced with what is different, the anxiety that results, spontaneous recourse to aggression in order to push back that anxiety—all of these are to be found in children, and probably in a good many adults as well. Whatever is different or foreign can be felt as a disturbing factor, hence a source of scandal. The attempt to wipe it out follows naturally. This is a primitive, virtually animal reaction, but it certainly goes deeper than we care to admit. We will have to give it more serious study instead of trying to sidestep it by optimistic moralizing. However that may be, the mechanism remains the same. By an accurate or a falsified characterization of the victim, the accuser attempts to explain and to justify his attitude and his behavior toward him.

Justifying Injustice

But what sort of attitude and behavior are these, that they need to be justified? Why does the accuser feel obliged to accuse in order to justify himself? Because he feels guilty toward his victim. Because he feels that his attitude and his behavior are essentially unjust and fraudulent. Here, in fact, we must turn the racist's argument inside out: he does not punish his victim because his victim deserves to be punished; he calls him guilty because he is already punished or, at best, because he, the accuser, is preparing to punish him.

Proof? In almost every case, the punishment has already been inflicted. The victim of racism is already living under the weight of disgrace and oppression. The racist does not aim his accusations at the mighty but at the vanquished. The Jew is already ostracized, the colonized is already colonized. In order to justify such punishment and misfortune, a process of rationalization is set in motion by which to explain away the ghetto and the colonial exploitation.

Very often, the precarious nature of the victim's life and the injustice of it are independent of the will of any individual. Racism is the objective counterpart of the victim's objective situation. Examples: women suffer because they have deserved to suffer; the Black man is a slave because he has been cast out. The individual can be tempted by this collective reasoning; it forms part of the values held by his peers and relieves him of the weight of any responsibility. Where everyone tolerates and condones scandal, scandal disappears.

Racism and Oppression

This is why racism accompanies almost every kind of oppression: racism is one of the best justifications of and symbols for oppression. I have found it in the colonial relationship, in anti-Semitism, and in oppression of the Black man. More or less explicitly, it is also found in the condition of the proletarian worker, the servant, and so on.

Of course it varies subtly, emerging differently from one social and historical context to another, from one form of oppression to another. The common denominator must not obscure the need, in each case, to look for the distinguishing features of each context: quite the contrary. As I have amply shown, the racist accusation, although it follows a relatively monotonous and banal pattern, should suggest something else—the precise context, the specific oppression that is the real cause of the racist alibi. The Black man is labeled congenitally good-for-nothing so that he can be kept in economic bondage; the colonized is tagged as unfit to handle anything technical so that colonization can last; the proletarian as politically and socially childish so that the domination of the property-owning classes can continue unchallenged. To come to the end of each particular form of racism, we will have to tackle colonization or the social and political structure of our societies.

The fact remains that we have discovered a fundamental mechanism, common to all racist reactions: the injustice of an oppressor toward the oppressed, the former's permanent aggression or the aggressive act he is getting ready to commit, must be justified. And isn't privilege one of the forms of permanent aggression, inflicted on a dominated man or group by a dominating man or group? How can any excuse be found for such disorder (source of so many advantages) if not by overwhelming the victim? Underneath its masks, racism is the racist's way of giving himself absolution.

The Definition Once Again

Now we can come back to the definition offered in the beginning to summarize the essential points of this commentary:

> *Racism is the generalized and final assigning of values to real or imaginary differences, to the accuser's benefit and at his victim's expense, in order to justify the former's own privileges or aggression.*

Memo on Fighting and Treating Racism

On the basis of the definition and the commentary relating to it, can we deduce a technique for taking action against racism?

I have been forced, as we have seen, to abandon once and for all that sociology of good intentions, or psychopathology, which looks on racism as a monstrous and incomprehensible aberration on the part of certain social groups or a sort of madness on the part of certain individuals. (The Nazi movement, for instance, is called an "inexplicable" phenomenon in twentieth-century Europe, and the racist's behavior is written off as vaguely pathological.) Whereas in fact there are bases for racism within the individual human being and within the social group. Racism is made operative by mechanisms that have their own special coherence. Any fight against racism must start with knowledge of these bases and these mechanisms and must act on them.

In other words, it is an information campaign that is called for, as well as a genuinely political fight.

The information and education campaign involves rethinking the notion of difference. For the racist, whether out of embarrassment or out of fear of the unknown, difference is bad and should be punished. It is paradoxical that neither the humanist nor the anti-racist contradicts this; both are content to deny that the difference exists—which is a way of dodging the issue. We must come around to recognizing certain differences among human beings and to showing that these differences are neither harmful nor scandalous.[6]

The political fight must be planned around a separate analysis of each context. Who benefits from the arguments justifying racism? What privilege or act of aggression does it prepare for or conceal? Then, if we really want to get at racism, we must tackle this concrete relationship, this implicit or explicit oppression.

Otherwise we will go on doing nothing more than expressing the indignation proper to sentimental anti-racism, which achieves as little as it costs.

APPENDIX B
WHAT IS RACISM?

Translated by Steve Martinot
Originally published in L'Encyclopaedia Universalis *(1972)*

It is not easy to find a definition for racism that everyone would accept. This is a bit surprising for a subject that is raised so often, in so many ways. But the difficulty arises from the fact that the essential foundation of racism, namely the concept of a pure race, when applied to humans, is ambiguous, and that it is impossible to find a clear example of it. This implies that racism is not a scientific theory, but rather a collection of opinions that are, in and of themselves, quite incoherent. That is, rather than derive from real descriptions about things exterior to those who express them, these opinions serve instead to justify attitudes and actions that are in turn motivated by fear of others and a desire to attack them. Ultimately, the purposes of this system are self-reassurance and self-affirmation, always gained to the detriment of the other. Ultimately, racism, as the use of biological differences, constitutes a particular case of a more general practice in which psychological or cultural differences, whether real or imaginary, work just as well. The point is that racism has a function (and unfortunately that function puts in question the possibility of its ever being totally eradicated). In any event, one can summarize all this as follows: *racism is a generalizing definition and valuation of biological differences, whether real or imaginary, to the advantage of the one defining and deploying them, and to the detriment of the one subjected to that act of definition, to the end of justifying (social or physical) hostility and assault*. The following discussion will both comment on and elucidate the reasoning behind this definition.

HISTORIC BENCHMARKS

The word *race* is of relatively recent use in French. It dates from the fifteenth century and derives from the Latin *ratio*,[1] which means, among other things, "chronological order." The logic of this latter notion has participated in the development of the modern biological concept of race. Race is now understood as a collection of biological and psychological characteristics that link the ancestors of a group with the contemporary group in a single line of descent. Originally a term used in animal breeding, the term *race* was not applied to humans until the beginning of the seventeenth century.

Racism as a doctrine is still more recent. For

the Spanish of the sixteenth century, it consisted of a "civilizing mission" on the American continents defined through the so-called natural inferiority and even "depravity" of the Native Americans. This was what authorized the Spanish conquest and settlement of the Americas and gave it legitimacy. In other words, racism, as the systematic attempt to justify the invasion and domination of a people proclaimed to be biologically inferior by another group that thereby judges itself superior, dates from the birth of colonialism. And it should be noted that the indigenous were not just considered inferior, which would not have been their "fault"; they were also defined as "depraved" and thus morally culpable, warranting punishment or at least sanction. For this did the "mission" of the White Man justify itself.

The African slave trade, which reached its acme in the seventeenth century, arises in correspondence with the first expositions of biological racism, arguments that Montesquieu himself saw fit to satirize.[2] Of course, one finds racist notions among some ancient authors, and even some first elements of a theoretical treatment. Aristotle, for instance, advocated a social order based on slavery and justified it by arguing that the "natural inferiority" of the Barbarians (non-Greeks) destined them to serve as slaves for Greeks. But these are, at best, only isolated remarks, often belied by actual events. The few cases in which biology is used to stigmatize were at the time only of secondary importance.

Anti-Semitism is certainly ancient, but that too was essentially based on religious, ethnic, or national ideas. Anti-Semitism as a racial doctrine only appears much later, with the partial social liberation of the Jews and their entry into forms of economic competition.

Only in the modern era do the systematic and pseudoscientific discourses of contemporary racism appear. Science alone could furnish the respectability that would properly guarantee that its thesis would be taken seriously. One of the initiators of racism, Joseph Arthur Gobineau (1816–1882), concluded from anatomical comparisons of brains and skulls that a member of the Huron could not begin to approach the cognitive capacity of a European. He is not the only one to think like that; some excellent minds are not far from sharing such opinions during that same period, or even earlier. For instance, the work of Linnaeus (1707–1778) and Buffon (1707–1788), who themselves were not beyond prejudice, paved the way for racism's pretense to being scientific—and, of course, Darwin has been used as another authority. By the end of the nineteenth century, the cultured mind of Europe was convinced that the human species is divided into superior and inferior races (see, for example, Ernest Renan and the anthropologist Paul Broca).[3]

This body of concepts, though only more or less clearly articulated, produced an extraordinary heritage. In France, the followers of Gobineau were violently anti-Jewish, though he himself was not exactly anti-Semitic. In Germany, his ideas were assimilated into its own anti-Semitic tradition (e.g., H. S. Chamberlain, 1855–1927), where they had the greatest influence, leading ultimately to genocide, concentration camps, and the deportation of entire populations. In Italy, fascism was the means sought to justify Italian hegemony over other peoples it had decided were inferior. In the Slavic countries, the pan-Slavic movements carefully searched through their own literature, cultural customs, and language for indications of a superiority they could use to authorize and even instigate their bloody pogroms. The Anglo-Saxon countries do not escape the disease; following the eugenics research of the Englishman Sir Francis Galton (1812–1911), some Anglo-Saxon thinkers met in London at the turn of the century to decide how to prevent the proliferation of other races, whom they thought posed a threat to the existence of the white race. In the United States, a veritable "ethnic cleansing" *[croisade ethnologique]* was in full swing. In South Africa, apartheid was made the foundation of that country's social institutions.

The syncretism of these diverse social doctrines brings to light a common element that transcends their specific local circumstances: in the name of biological superiority, one human group seeks to advance and affirm itself against and through others, and believes itself justified in deploying any and all means possible to do this, including violence and murder.

OPINIONS, ATTITUDES, AND BEHAVIOR

To assert racial superiority, one must first assume the existence of human races. The racist stance must firmly underwrite the idea that there exist pure races, that these are superior to others, and that this superiority authorizes political and historical hegemony. These three points have been submitted to widespread criticism.

First, the vast majority of real human groups are the products of prior human admixture *[métissage]*, to the point where it is practically impossible to delineate a "pure race." It is already very difficult to classify human groups according to biological criteria, since those criteria are themselves imprecise. Ultimately, the constant development of humanity as a species and the provisional character of human groupings render any attempt to define race on stable ethnic grounds an illusion.

In short, *the very concept of biological purity for human groups is unfounded.* It is, after all, a term used in animal breeding, in which race, conceived as pure, is nevertheless something achieved only through controlled procedures. When applied to humans, the notion of biological group gets confused with linguistic or national group. This was seen in the case of the Aryan idea, a concept exploited by Gobineau and the Nazis. The fantasy of purity is possible only as an implicit reference within such a notion.

In any case, suppose that a purity exists—how would one connect biological purity and superiority? And of what does this latter consist? If, hypothetically, a biological superiority does exist in some connection with ethnic characteristics, it still does not explain how that conditions the psychological or cultural superiority on which racism so emphatically insists.

Furthermore, supposing that there might be certain real superiorities, whether provisional or substantial, whether linked to actual purity or not, why would they legitimate political hegemony or social advantage?

It is clear that this is not a question of established scientific fact but rather of political choice, a program and a desire to establish political hegemony while falsely supporting it on biological or cultural grounds.

Thus, a final and insurmountable paradox emerges from within racism itself: the provisional nature of ethnic or cultural groups, of peoples and nations, renders any political program based on definite ethnic or cultural characteristics illegitimate.

In conclusion, racism is not a scientific theory but a pseudotheory, a body of opinion devoid of logical connections with biological notions, which are themselves conceptually vague.

ATTEMPTS AT JUSTIFICATION

It is now clear why a definition of racism is so difficult. The first principle of racism—the concept of race applied to humans—is an ambiguous notion; or rather, it is a notion to which one cannot assign a clearly defined object or referent. Hence, the thinking that follows from this dubious notion must itself be dubious and essentially incoherent in its reasoning.

However, the relationship between the frailty of racism's foundations in either science or reality and the force of the judgments derived from it is not without interest. The passion that racism engenders, its tenacity and extensiveness, compared to the confusion, the casuistry, and the contradictions that are its stock in trade, should prove, if proof were needed, that the foundation of racism is not in reasoning but in affect and self-interest. We must reverse our approach and use racist discourse to reflect on those who uphold and speak it, rather than on those it is about. Far from being knowledge, or constituting a scientific theory by which to govern one's thought and behavior, racism relies on mental constructs and rationalizations to justify itself, which are themselves fueled and driven by the psychological needs of its own practices and projects.

Racist thinking focuses on biological differences, whether real or presumed, from which it derives practices that it then seeks to legitimate, and which produce, in turn, a politics and a social philosophy, sometimes even a metaphysics. Thus, for Whites, the color and physical characteristics of Black people, which are made to signify a biological inferiority, constitute the very authorization to preside over them. The Jew, once described in biological terms, becomes an "evil being," one who is both cursed and the carrier of worse catastrophes for others.

But difference, whether biological or otherwise, is only a point of departure, a stage upon which the drama endlessly unfolds. To make its case, racist thinking will stop at nothing. It will enlist a "cephalic index" to be the measure of mental and spiritual capacity; or else it will foreground a particular psychological aspect of an individual's comportment and use it to characterize an entire group; or else it will claim to have discovered a group characteristic that it then attributes to each member separately. Even when the trait is real, no such generalization is ever legitimate, let alone the signification given to it. But in every case, whether the difference addressed be biological, psychological, cultural, or social, its meaning will be to the advantage of the racist.

To look at the matter in this light puts in question what is at stake in the term *racism*. We confront a structure that is more extensive and profound than at first suspected. If one sought to signify a theory of human races, it would have been more appropriate to use the term *raciology*. But the meanings projected by racist discourse are not the prime concern; its real issue is its implicit condemnation and rejection of individuals or groups for belonging to another race. It is not just a question of describing biological difference but of attacking a people or a group under the cover of that biological description. Thus, it would be more appropriate to call it *ethnophobia*. This latter term would offer itself to a very broad range of human phenomena, of which racism would be only a single, and perhaps temporary, variety.

PSYCHOLOGICAL AND SOCIAL MOTIVATIONS

But the extensiveness, the similarity of practices that are engendered in diverse social groups, and the tenacity of the opinions and the attitudes that sustain it, all suggest that the many forms of racism respond to similar individual and collective motivations. That is, racism unfolds on both an individual and an institutional level, implying that both its psychological and its social functions must be understood.

Aggressiveness against others, in acts or in words, always has a need to justify itself. The two main ways through which it does this are fear and self-interest.

Our fear of others comes to us from the distant past, from an epoch in which one lived in distrust, as a necessary stance toward those who were stronger or more cunning, who might prey upon one, take one's goods or one's wife, condemn one to hunger or to humiliation or even to death. The Other is the unknown, through whom everything happens—above all, bad things.

The passage to racism is easy: one must defend oneself against this Other who is strange and foreign and, more to the point, preempt his attacks by attacking first. If his mere existence is threatening, then he must be bad in himself, which in turn justifies hating him. To assuage this fear of the Other, racism provides explanations and reassurances; most of all, it excuses and legitimizes one's attacks.

In terms of fear, racist conduct translates into two complementary gestures: a refusal of the Other and an affirmation of oneself through that refusal, whose common end is to fortify the racist against the Other. Or, to put it in psychoanalytic terms, racism strengthens the individual and collective ego. Of course, it is done in bad faith, however temporarily, and with unavoidable injustice; that is, it is done in a domain in which morality is necessarily in retreat and the mythic given easy victory.

A similar structure comes into play with respect to self-interest, namely, an aggressive hostility and the utilization of a biological or other difference (whether real or imaginary) in a quasi-mythic manner to justify that hostility.

Racism was the ideology of the slave trade and of nascent colonialism. The biological argument was first used in a systematic fashion by the Spanish nobility in their struggle against the Jews who had converted to Christianity, and who had thus gained the same rights as they. They fell back upon the notion of an incommensurable difference of "blood" as a way to rationalize the dismantling of that social equality. The Nazis replayed the same idea to justify their expansion of Germany. Because nascent capitalism needed to provide itself with herds of manual laborers, as if of cattle, it demanded that laborers be considered as such. The merchants, doctors, or lawyers of liberal society defend their own interests with the same kind of arguments when the competition of Blacks and Jews begins to be a problem, because racist or anti-Semitic comportment is available to them.

There is no real contradiction between these two modes of justification; indeed, they are often quite inseparable. Why are Swiss or French citizens of median or modest means so often racist with respect to foreign travelers who come to fill labor functions that are indispensable to the economy of their country? Because they are afraid; these citizens are obscurely dominated by an anxiety toward these people who are different from themselves and who threaten to disturb the social routines to which they are attached. At the same time, they are well aware that the immigrants are relegated to the dirtiest jobs, for the worst pay and with doubtful social benefits. And this but neatly bestows a legitimacy on their own privileges, limited though they may be.

One aspect of racist thinking brings these threads together into a form of coherence: *the tendency to generalize and to consider things in absolute terms.* For each individual who is denigrated and condemned, there must be a condemnation of his or her group as well. And what better guarantee of security can one find than an inferiority without appeal? The individual does not exist as such; he belongs to a deleterious group, whose debasement he cannot escape. So degraded a people will never again lift their head; a group so reduced will be that way forever, since their very being condemns them.

But what must be equally taken into account are the many ways racism unfolds. While the functions of racism are anxiety alleviation and ideological distraction, its general structure opens the possibility of many different specific forms manifested according to circumstance and the particular groups involved.

It is therefore necessary to describe each different racist situation in its specificity. The concrete manner in which Black workers are treated, at a particular time and place, will not be the same as the way immigrant workers from Turkey, or from other parts of Europe, are treated. The Algerian War weighs heavily on the image of Algerian workers. As for anti-Semitism, while it is a form of racism, it nevertheless possesses its own specific object.

But this concrete diversity must not hide the fact that the phenomenon has a general nature that is discernibly at work in different times and places, and in very different societies. While one can perhaps link certain types of racism to industrial capitalist development and to the class struggle, for example, it would be meaningless to tie all forms of racism to it, as some people have been inspired to do.

Since the human mind has certain tendencies toward being racist, it is possible that such comportment will be around a long time. However, the alibi furnished by biological differences to rationalize rejection of the Other, with its hostile aggressions, has not always been in existence. One might hope it will give way to other modes of social relations. Biology has long been a convenient explanation for the anguish of humanity. But with the global unification of the planet, and the self-affirmation of the peoples of Africa, Asia, and the Americas, perhaps the idea of considering others inferior because of skin color, the form of the nose, or certain character traits will finally become untenable. But biological exclusion only took the place of a prior religious exclusion; it is not impossible that it will only be replaced in turn by political exclusion, for example. Its fundamental machinery and structure will not necessarily disappear with it.

How is one to struggle effectively against racism? Moral indignation and attempts at persuasion have shown themselves to be clearly insufficient. One must take full account of racism's roots in fear, in financial insecurity, in economic avarice, which are in humans the sources of aggressivity and a tendency toward domination. One must struggle against such aggressions and dominations, and prevent them. It is racism that is natural and anti-racism that is not; anti-racism can only be something that is acquired, as all that is cultural is acquired, at the end of long and arduous struggles, which are never free from the possibility of being reversed.

APPENDIX C
THE RELATIVITY OF PRIVILEGE

Translated by Howard Greenfield
Reprinted from Albert Memmi, The Colonizer and the Colonized *(Boston: Beacon Press, 1965), 10–17.*
Originally published as Portrait du colonisé, précédé de portrait du colonisateur *(Paris: Corréa, 1957).*

Naturally, not all Europeans in the colonies are potentates or possess thousands of acres or run the government. Many of them are victims of the masters of colonization, exploited by these masters in order to protect interests that do not often coincide with their own. In addition, social relationships are almost never balanced. Contrary to everything that we like to think, the small colonizer is actually, in most cases, a supporter of colonialists and an obstinate defender of colonial privileges. Why?

Solidarity of fellow man with fellow man? A defensive reaction, an expression of anxiety by a minority living in the midst of a hostile majority? Partly. But during the peak of the colonial process, protected by the police, the army, and an air force always ready to step in, Europeans in the colonies were not sufficiently afraid to explain such unanimity. It is certain that they were not just-minded. It is true that the small colonizer himself would have a fight to carry on, a liberation to bring about, if he were not so seriously fooled by his own naïveté and blinded by history. But I do not believe that gullibility can rest on a complete illusion or can completely govern human conduct. If the small colonizer defends the colonial system so vigorously, it is because he benefits from it to some extent. His gullibility lies in the fact that to protect his very limited interests, he protects other infinitely more important ones, of which he is, incidentally, the victim. But, though dupe and victim, he also gets his share.

However, privilege is something relative. To different degrees every colonizer is privileged, at least comparatively so, ultimately to the detriment of the colonized. If the privileges of the masters of colonization are striking, the lesser privileges of the small colonizer, even the smallest, are very numerous. Every act of his daily life places him in a relationship with the colonized, and with each act his fundamental advantage is demonstrated. If he is in trouble with the law, the police and even justice will be more lenient toward him. If he needs assistance from the government, it will not be difficult; red tape will be cut, a window will be reserved for him where there is a shorter line so he will have a shorter wait. Does he need a job? Must he take an examination for it? Jobs and positions will be reserved for him in advance; the tests will be given in his language, causing disqualifying difficulties for the colonized. Can he be so blind or so blinded that he can never see that, given equal material circumstances, economic class, or capabilities, he always receives preferred treatment? How could he help looking back from time to time to see all the colonized, sometimes former schoolmates or colleagues, whom he has so greatly outpaced?

Lastly, should he ask for or have need of anything, he only has to show his face to be prejudged favorably by those in the colony who count. He enjoys the preference and respect of the colonized themselves, who grant him more than those who are the best of their own people; who, for example, have more faith in his word than in that of their own population. From the time of his birth, he possesses a qualification independent of his personal merits or his actual class. He is part of the group of colonizers whose values are sovereign. The colony follows the cadence of his traditional holidays, even religious holidays, and not those of the inhabitants. The weekly day of rest is that of his native country; his nation's flag flies over the monuments, his mother tongue permits social communication. Even his dress, his accent, and his manners are eventually imitated by the colonized. The colonizer partakes of an elevated world from which he automatically reaps the privileges.

It is also their concrete economic and psychological position within the colonial society in relation to the colonized on one hand, and to the colonizers on the other hand, that accounts for the traits of the other human groups—those who are neither colonizers nor colonized. Among these are the nationals of other powers (Italians, Maltese of Tunisia), candidates for assimilation (the majority of Jews), the recently assimilated (Corsicans in Tunisia, Spaniards in Algeria). To these can be added the representatives of the authorities recruited among the colonized themselves.

The poverty of the Italians or Maltese is such that it may seem ludicrous to speak of privileges in connection with them. Nonetheless, if they are often in want, the small crumbs that are automatically accorded them contribute toward differentiating them—substantially separating them from the colonized. To whatever extent favored as compared to the colonized masses, they tend to establish relationships of the colonizer-colonized nature. At the same time, not corresponding to the colonizing group, not having the same role as theirs in colonial society, they each stand out in their own way.

All these nuances are easily understandable in an analysis of their relationship with colonial life. If the Italians in Tunisia have always envied the French for their legal and administrative privileges, they are nevertheless in a better situation than the colonized. They are protected by international laws and an extremely watchful consulate under constant observation by an attentive mother country. Often, far from being rejected by the colonizer, it is they who hesitate between integration and loyalty to their homeland. Moreover, the same European origin, a common religion, and a majority of identical customs bring them sentimentally closer to the colonizer. The results are definite advantages that the colonized certainly does not have: better job opportunities, less insecurity against total misery and illness, less precarious schooling, and a certain esteem on the part of the colonizer accompanied by an almost respectable dignity. It will be understood that, as much as they may be outcasts in an absolute sense, their behavior vis-à-vis the colonized has much in common with that of the colonizer.

On the other hand, benefiting from colonization by proxy only, the Italians are much less removed from the colonized people than are the French. They do not have that stilted, formal relationship with them, that tone that always smacks of a master addressing his slave, which the French cannot entirely shed. In contrast to the French, almost all the Italians speak the language of the colonized, make long-lasting friendships and even—a particularly revealing sign—mixed marriages with them. To sum up, having no special reason to do so, Italians do not maintain a great distance between themselves and the colonized. The same analysis would apply, subject to some minor differences, to the Maltese.

The situation of the Jewish population—eternally hesitant candidates refusing assimilation—can be viewed in a similar light. Their constant and very justifiable ambition is to escape from their colonized condition, an additional burden in an already oppressive status. To that end, they endeavor to resemble the colonizer in the frank hope that he may cease to consider them different from him. Hence their efforts to forget the past, to change collective habits, and their enthusiastic adoption of Western language, culture, and customs. But if the colonizer does not always openly discourage these candidates to develop that resemblance, he never permits them to attain it either. Thus, they live in painful and constant ambiguity. Rejected by the colonizer, they share in part the physical conditions of the colonized and have a communion of interests with him; on the other hand, they reject the values of the colonized as belonging to a decayed world from which they eventually hope to escape.

The recently assimilated place themselves in a considerably superior position to the average colonizer. They push a colonial mentality to excess, display proud disdain for the colonized, and continually show off their borrowed rank, which often belies a vulgar brutality and avidity. Still too impressed by their privileges, they savor them and defend them with fear and harshness, and when colonization is imperiled, they provide it with its most dynamic defenders, its shock troops, and sometimes its instigators.

The representatives of the authorities, cadres, policemen, etc., recruited from among the colonized form a category of the colonized that attempts to escape from its political and social condition. But in so doing, by choosing to place themselves in the colonizer's service to protect his interests exclusively, they end up by adopting his ideology, even with regard to their own values and their own lives.

Having been fooled to the point of accepting the inequities of his position, even at times profiting from this unjust system, the colonized still finds his situation more of a burden than anything else. Their contempt may be only a compensation for their misery, just as European anti-Semitism is so often a convenient outlet for misery. Such is the history of the pyramid of petty tyrants: each one, socially oppressed by the one more powerful than he, always finds a less powerful one on whom to lean, and becomes a tyrant in his turn. What revenge and what pride for a non-colonized small-time carpenter to walk side by side with an Arab laborer carrying a board and a few nails on his head! All have at least this profound satisfaction of being negatively better than the colonized: they are never completely engulfed in the abasement into which colonialism drives them.

APPENDIX D

THE MYTHIC PORTRAIT OF THE COLONIZED

Translated by Howard Greenfield
Reprinted from Albert Memmi, The Colonizer and the Colonized *(Boston: Beacon Press, 1965), 79–91.*
Originally published as Portrait du colonisé, précédé de portrait du colonisateur *(Paris: Corréa, 1957).*

Just as the bourgeoisie proposes an image of the proletariat, the existence of the colonizer requires that an image of the colonized be suggested. These images become excuses without which the presence and conduct of a colonizer, and that of a bourgeois, would seem shocking. But the favored image becomes a myth precisely because it suits them too well.

Let us imagine, for the sake of this portrait and accusation, the often-cited trait of laziness. It seems to receive unanimous approval of colonizers from Liberia to Laos, via the Maghreb. It is easy to see to what extent this description is useful. It occupies an important place in the dialectics exalting the colonizer and humbling the colonized. Furthermore, it is economically fruitful.

Nothing could better justify the colonizer's privileged position than his industry, and nothing could better justify the colonized's destitution than his indolence. The mythical portrait of the colonized therefore includes an unbelievable laziness, and that of the colonizer, a virtuous taste for action. At the same time the colonizer suggests that employing the colonized is not very profitable, thereby authorizing his unreasonable wages.

It may seem that colonization would profit by employing experienced personnel. Nothing is less true. A qualified worker existing among the colonizers earns three or four times more than does the colonized, while he does not produce three or four times as much, either in quantity or in quality. It is more advantageous to use three of the colonized than one European. Every firm needs specialists, of course, but only a minimum of them, and the colonizer imports or recruits experts among his own kind. In addition, there is the matter of the special attention and legal protection required by a European worker. The colonized, however, is only asked for his muscles; he is so poorly evaluated that three or four can be taken on for the price of one European.

From listening to him, on the other hand, one finds that the colonizer is not so displeased with that laziness, whether supposed or real. He talks of it with amused affability, he jokes about it, he takes up all the usual expressions, perfects them, and invents others. Nothing can describe well enough the extraordinary deficiency of the colonized. He becomes lyrical about it, in a negative way. The colonized doesn't let grass grow under his feet, but a tree, and what a tree! A eucalyptus, an American centenarian oak! A tree? No, a forest!

But, one will insist, is the colonized truly lazy? To tell the truth, the question is poorly stated. Besides having to define a point of reference, a norm, varying from one people to another, can one accuse an entire people of laziness? It can be suspected of individuals, even many of them in a single group. One can wonder, if their output is mediocre, whether malnutrition, low wages, a closed future, a ridiculous conception of a role in society does not make the colonized uninterested in his work. What is suspect is that the accusation is not directed solely at the farm laborer or slum resident but also at the professor, engineer, or physician who does the same number of hours of work as his colonizer colleagues; indeed, all individuals of the colonized group are accused. Essentially, the independence of the accusation from any sociological or historical conditions makes it suspect.

In fact, the accusation has nothing to do with an objective notation, therefore subject to possible changes, but with an institution. By his accusation the colonizer establishes the colonized as being lazy. He decides that laziness is constitutional in the very nature of the colonized. It becomes obvious that the colonized, whatever he may undertake, whatever zeal he may apply, could never be anything but lazy. This always brings us back to racism, which is the substantive expression, to the accuser's benefit, of a real or imaginary trait of the accused.

It is possible to proceed with the same analysis for each of the features found in the colonized.

Whenever the colonizer states, in his language, that the colonized is a weakling, he suggests thereby that this deficiency requires protection. From this comes the concept of a protectorate. It is in the colonized's own interest that he be excluded from management functions and that those heavy responsibilities be reserved for the colonizer. Whenever the colonizer adds, in order not to fall prey to anxiety, that the colonized is a wicked, backward person with evil, thievish, somewhat sadistic instincts, he thus justifies his police and his legitimate severity. After all, he must defend himself against the dangerous foolish acts of the irresponsible, and at the same time—what meritorious concern!—protect him against himself! It is the same for the colonized's lack of desires, his ineptitude for comfort, science, progress, his astonishing familiarity with poverty. Why should the colonizer worry about things that hardly trouble the interested party? It would be, he adds with dark and insolent philosophy, doing him a bad turn if he subjected him to the disadvantages of civilization. After all, remember that wisdom is Eastern; let us accept, as he does, the colonized's wretchedness. The same reasoning is also true for the colonized's notorious ingratitude; the colonizer's acts of charity are wasted, the improvements the colonizer has made are not appreciated. It is impossible to save the colonized from this myth—a portrait of wretchedness has been indelibly engraved.

It is significant that this portrait requires nothing else. It is difficult, for instance, to reconcile most of these features and then to proceed to synthesize them objectively. One can hardly see how the colonized can be simultaneously inferior and wicked, lazy and backward.

What is more, the traits ascribed to the colonized are incompatible with one another, though this does not bother his prosecutor. He is depicted as frugal, sober, without many desires, and, at the same time, he consumes disgusting quantities of meat, fat, alcohol, anything; as a coward who is afraid of suffering and as a brute who is not checked by any inhibitions of civilization. It is additional proof that it is useless to seek this consistency anywhere except in the colonizer himself. At the basis of the entire construction, one finally finds a common motive: the colonizer's economic and basic needs, which he substitutes for logic, and which shape and explain each of the traits he assigns to the colonized. In the last analysis, these traits are all advantageous to the colonizer, even those that at first sight seem damaging to him.

The point is that the colonized means little to the colonizer. Far from wanting to understand him as he really is, the colonizer is preoccupied with making him undergo this urgent change. The mechanism of this remolding of the colonized is revealing in itself. It consists, in the first place, of a series of negations. The colonized is not this, is not that. He is never considered in a positive light; or if he is, the quality that is conceded is the result of a psychological or ethical failing. Thus it is with Arab hospitality, which is difficult to consider as a negative characteristic. If one pays attention, one discovers that the praise comes from tourists, visiting Europeans, and not colonizers, i.e., Europeans who have settled down in the colony. As soon as he is settled, the European no longer takes advantage of this hospitality but cuts off intercourse and contributes to the barriers that plague the colonized. He rapidly changes palette to portray the colonized, who becomes jealous, withdrawn, intolerant, and fanatical. What happens to the famous hospitality? Since he cannot deny it, the colonizer then brings into play the shadows and describes the disastrous consequences.

This hospitality is a result of the colonized's irresponsibility and extravagance, since he has no notion of foresight or economy. From the wealthy down to the fellah, the festivities are wonderful and bountiful—but what happens afterward? The colonized ruins himself, borrows and finally pays with someone else's money! Does one speak, on the other hand, of the modesty of the colonized's life? Of his not less well known lack of needs? It is no longer a proof of wisdom but of stupidity—as if, then, every recognized or invented trait had to be an indication of negativity.

Thus, one after another, all the qualities that make a man of the colonized crumble away. The humanity of the colonized, rejected by the colonizer, becomes opaque. It is useless, he asserts, to try to forecast the colonized's actions. ("They are unpredictable!" "With them, you never know!") It seems to him that a strange and disturbing impulsiveness controls the colonized. The colonized must indeed be very strange, if he remains so mysterious after years of living with the colonizer.

Another sign of the colonized's depersonalization is what one might call the mark of the plural. The colonized is never characterized in an individual manner; he is entitled only to drown in an anonymous collectivity. ("They are this." "They are all the same.") If a colonized servant does not come in one morning, the colonizer will not say that she is ill, or that she is cheating, or that she is tempted not to abide by an oppressive contract. (Seven days a week; colonized domestics rarely enjoy the one day off a week granted to others.) He will say, "You can't count on them." It is not just a grammatical expression. He refuses to consider personal, private occurrences in his maid's life; that life in a specific sense does not interest him, and his maid does not exist as an individual.

Finally, the colonizer denies the colonized the most precious right granted to most men: liberty. Living conditions imposed on the colonized by colonization make no provision for it; indeed, they ignore it. The colonized has no way out of his state of woe—neither a legal outlet (naturalization) nor a religious outlet (conversion). The colonized is not free to choose between being colonized or not being colonized.

What is left of the colonized at the end of this stubborn effort to dehumanize him? He is surely no longer an alter ego of the colonizer. He is hardly a human being. He tends rapidly toward becoming an object. As an end, in the colonizer's supreme ambition, he should exist only as a function of the needs of the colonizer, i.e., be transformed into a pure colonized.

The extraordinary efficiency of this operation is obvious. One does not have a serious obligation toward an animal or an object. It is then easily understood that the colonizer can indulge in such shocking attitudes and opinions. A colonized driving a car is a sight to which the colonizer refuses to become accustomed; he denies him all normality. An accident, even a serious one, overtaking the colonized almost makes him laugh. A machine-gun burst into a crowd of colonized causes him merely to shrug his shoulders. Even a native mother weeping over the death of her son or a native woman weeping for her husband reminds him only vaguely of the grief of a mother or a wife. Those desperate cries, those unfamiliar gestures would be enough to freeze his compassion even if it were aroused. An author was recently humorously telling us how rebelling natives were driven like game toward huge cages. The fact that someone had conceived and then dared build those cages, and even more, that reporters had been allowed to photograph the fighting, certainly proves that the spectacle had contained nothing human.

Madness for destroying the colonized having originated with the needs of the colonizers, it is not surprising that it conforms so well to them, that it seems to confirm and justify the colonizer's conduct. More surprising, more harmful perhaps, is the echo that it excites in the colonized himself. Constantly confronted with this image of himself, set forth and imposed on all institutions and in every human contact, how could the colonized help reacting to his portrait? It cannot leave him indifferent and remain a veneer that, like an insult, blows with the wind. He ends up recognizing it as one would a detested nickname that has become a familiar description. The accusation disturbs him and worries him even more because he admires and fears his powerful accuser. "Is he not partly right?" he mutters. "Are we not all a little guilty after all? Lazy, because we have so many idlers? Timid, because we let ourselves be oppressed." Willfully created and spread by the colonizer, this mythical and degrading portrait ends up by being accepted and lived with to a certain extent by the colonized. It thus acquires a certain amount of reality and contributes to the true portrait of the colonized.

This process is not unknown. It is a hoax. It is common knowledge that the ideology of a governing class is adopted in large measure by the governed classes. Now, every ideology of combat includes as an integral part of itself a conception of the adversary. By agreeing to this ideology, the dominated classes practically confirm the role assigned to them. This explains, inter alia, the relative stability of societies; oppression is tolerated willy-nilly by the oppressed themselves. In colonial relationships, domination is imposed by people upon people but the pattern remains the same. The characterization and role of the colonized occupies a choice place in colonialist ideology, a characterization that is neither true to life nor in itself incoherent, but necessary and inseparable within that ideology. It is one to which the colonized gives his troubled and partial, but undeniable, assent.

There is only a particle of truth in the fashionable notions of "dependency complex," "colonizability," etc. There undoubtedly exists—at some point in its evolution—a certain adherence of the colonized to colonization. However, this adherence is the result of colonization and not its cause. It arises after and not before colonial occupation. In order for the colonizer to be the complete master, it is not enough for him to be so in actual fact, but he must also believe in its legitimacy. In order for that legitimacy to be completed, it is not enough for the colonized to be a slave; he must also accept his role. The bond between colonizer and colonized is thus destructive and creative. It destroys and re-creates the two partners of colonization into colonizer and colonized. One is disfigured into an oppressor, a partial, unpatriotic, and treacherous being, worrying only about his privileges and their defense; the other, into an oppressed creature, whose development is broken and who compromises by his defeat.

Just as the colonizer is tempted to accept his part, the colonized is forced to accept being colonized.

It would have been too good if that mythical portrait had remained a pure illusion, a look at the colonized that would only have softened the colonizer's bad conscience. However, impelled by the same needs that created it, it cannot fail to be expressed in actual conduct, in active and constructive behavior. (And the same can be said for anti-Semitism.)

Since the colonized is presumed a thief, he must in fact be guarded against. (Being suspect by definition, why should he not be guilty?) Some laundry was stolen (a frequent incident in these sunny lands, where the laundry dries in the open air and mocks those who are naked), and who but the first colonized seen in that vicinity can be guilty? Since it may be he, they go to his home and take him to the police station. (The same happens to Gypsies, who camp at the edge of the city.)

"Some injustice!" retorts the colonizer. "One time out of two, we hit it right. And, in any case, the thief is a colonized; if we don't find him in the first hut, he'll be in the second one."

This conduct, which is common to colonizers as a group, thus becomes what can be called a social institution. In other words, it defines and establishes concrete situations that close in on the colonized, weigh on him until they bend his conduct and leave their marks on his face. Generally speaking, these are situations of inadequacy. The ideological aggression that tends to dehumanize and then deceive the colonized finally corresponds to concrete situations that lead to the same result. To be deceived to some extent already, to endorse the myth and then adapt to it, is to be acted upon by it. That myth is furthermore supported by a very solid organization, a government and a judicial system fed and renewed by the colonizer's historic, economic, and cultural needs. Even if he were insensitive to calumny and scorn, even if he shrugged his shoulders at insults and jostling, how could the colonized escape the low wages, the agony of his culture, the law that rules him from birth until death?

Just as the colonized cannot escape the colonialist hoax, he could not avoid those situations that create real inadequacy. To a certain extent, the true portrait of the colonized is a function of this relationship. Reversing a previous formula, it can be stated that colonization creates the colonized, just as we have seen that it creates the colonizer.

NOTES

FOREWORD

1. I made an attempt myself at a definition some years ago in "Racisms," an essay in *Anatomy of Racism,* David Goldberg, ed. (Minneapolis: University of Minnesota Press, 1990), 3–17. The standard contemporary sociological account in the United States is M. Omi and H. Winant, *Racial Formation in the United States: From the 1960s to the 1990s,* 2d ed. (New York: Routledge, 1994). An especially important recent contribution is Jorge García, "The Heart of Racism," *Journal of Social Philosophy* 27, no. 1 (spring 1996): 5–45; this essay is also included in *Racism: Key Concepts in Critical Theory,* Leonard Harris, ed. (New York: Humanities Press, 1999).

INTRODUCTION

1. For much biographical material on Memmi, I am indebted to Judith Roumani, whose brief but insightful

autobiographical sketch is very informative. Memmi himself also includes autobiographical material in this present work and in others. See Judith Roumani, *Albert Memmi* (Philadelphia: Celfan Editions, 1987).

2. W. E. B. Du Bois, *The Souls of Black Folk* (Greenwich: Fawcett, 1961), 16–18.

3. As a concrete example, we have the instance of the public session of President Clinton's Commission on Race Relations in San Jose, California, in 1998 (*San Francisco Chronicle,* February 11, 1998). At this meeting, two types of disruption occurred. One was by a number of poor and working-class Black people who claimed the problem wasn't race relations but racism and accused the panel of having excluded those who most suffered from it, *viz.,* people like themselves. The other was by a White man who accused the entire project of "white bashing," of blaming whites in the present for what happened in the past. The problem, he said, isn't white racism but minority complaints about their own situation, the racism of those who blame everything on the white race. Clearly, a dialogue between these two sides would be very difficult. One seeks to call attention to a hierarchical system of racialization by which their lives have been truncated; the other defensively denies the existence of racial hierarchy itself.

4. This is the case with the contemporary criminalization of people of color. The police legitimize their arrest of a disproportionate number of Black men through suspect profiles, yet those profiles are constructed from their own statistics. Prosecutors charge Black men with felonies for which Whites would get lesser charges, as a slow process of disenfranchisement. Affirmative action programs designed to deal with past discrimination and inequality are being dismantled because they allegedly foster "reverse discrimination," as if their mere existence had changed the entire structure of power relations. Racial minorities are called the real racists because they are the ones who bring it up. In short, the issue is immaterial; it is the ability to levy a charge against the other that matters.

5. Memmi sketches certain aspects of this in his novel *The Scorpion.* See Albert Memmi, *The Scorpion; or, The Imaginary Confession,* trans. Eleanor Levieux (New York:

Grossman, 1971); originally published as *Le Scorpion, ou la Confession imaginaire* (Paris: Gallimard, 1969).

6. Memmi depicts facets of this dynamic in his first novel. See Albert Memmi, *The Pillar of Salt,* trans. Edouard Roditi (Chicago: J. P. O'Hara, 1955); originally published as *La statue de sel,* preface by Albert Camus (Paris: Corréa, 1953).

7. In *The Scorpion,* the narrator discovers and reads the journal pages that an older brother had written and thrown in a desk drawer. The narrator takes issue and dialogues monologically with the brother's account of various things. Interspersed with the journal are the pages of a novel that retells in still other terms some of the events contained in the journal. *The Scorpion* is thus a novel within a novel, and a novel about plural perspectives in a multicultural environment.

8. See, in this regard, M. M. Bakhtin, *The Dialogic Imagination,* trans. Michael Holquist (Austin: University of Texas Press, 1981). The question of who speaks for themselves and who is spoken for by others is part of the problematic of the double consciousness. Racialization comes from elsewhere, from social structures that determine who will benefit and who will be marginalized; under its marginalization, how is one to speak for oneself if the discourses by which one can know oneself come from others? Indeed, to be spoken for means to be silenced, even when one speaks. This is the problem that Gayatri Spivak addresses in her essay "Can the Subaltern Speak?" in *Marxism and the Interpretation of Culture,* ed. Larry Grossman and Cary Nelson (Urbana: University of Illinois Press, 1988).

9. In this sense, it is reminiscent of Franz Kafka, *The Trial.* In Kafka's novel, there is a charge, never specified, against which the main character K has to defend himself; his failure to do so is a foregone conclusion. The novel can be seen as an allegory about anti-Semitism.

10. Theodore Allen argues that English indentured servitude was a form of chattel because the contract became the primary factor of the labor relation, and the laborer could be "assigned" to others through sale or lease of the contract, like property. See Theodore W. Allen, *The Invention of the White Race* (New York: Verso, 1997), 97ff. In addition, the absence of contracts for

Africans brought the auction markets into existence, as opposed to contract trading for English bond-laborers. The auction markets transformed African-American labor into calculable wealth by establishing price standards, similar to stock market operations today.

11. Bacon's rebellion marked a major turning point in the process of racialization. In that rebellion, masses of English and African-American bond-laborers appeared under arms together. In its wake, the colonial elite restructured society to prevent further common cause against itself by transforming the class status of White bond-laborers and small farmers. Poor Whites were given guard (vigilante) duty against runaway African-Americans, and special statutes were passed inculcating fear of "Negro rebellion," thus racializing the very act of protest or rebellion. Poor Whites were thus molded into an intermediary control stratum between the plantations and the African-American slaves, in the name of defensive "White solidarity" against an internal enemy.

12. Cf. William W. Hening, ed., *Statutes at Large: A Collection of All the Laws of Virginia* (Richmond, Va., 1809).

DESCRIPTION

1. [Even David Duke, once head of the Ku Klux Klan, a Nazi sympathizer, and a supporter of revisionist history of Nazi genocide, has claimed not to be a racist. His claim is that there is a racism against White people, of which affirmative action is a manifestation, and what he is struggling for is equal rights for Whites. In twisting things so that the Whites become the victims of a Black seizure of the society, he creates a mythology in which it is impossible that he be a racist. This mythology, that the minority black population has made war upon the majority white population, aided by the government, and against which he is demanding equal rights for Whites, is simply an update of that advanced by D. W. Griffith in his film *Birth of a Nation*. See Tyler Bridges, *The Rise of David Duke* (Jackson: University Press of Mississippi, 1994), 137–38.

Rick Oltman, one of the leaders of the anti-immigrant movement in California for Proposition 187, makes a similar statement in which he claims he cannot be racist in opposing immigrants, whom he sees as having seized the benefits of this society from its citizens, because he is in defense of Americans. *San Francisco Chronicle* (March 30, 1994): 11.—Trans.]

2. Albert Jacquard, "À la recherche d'un contenu pour le mot race" [In search of a meaning for the word "race"], in *Le Racism, mythes et science,* Maurice Olender, Pierre Birnbaum, et al., eds., Collection de la Science (Brussels: Complexe, 1981).

3. [Memmi often uses the masculine gender as the universal case. In French, the traditional terms *man* and *he* still function in that capacity. There have been some attempts by the feminist movements to modify French in order to attentuate the male or patriarchal bias of the language, just as there have been in English. But gender is much more strongly marked and explicit in French than it is in English. Thus, greater possibilities of deploying gender-neutral language exist in English than in French. The question of gender bias arises from within the language itself, whose political and ethical dimensions I think it is important to note. Memmi does include the continued exclusion and derogation of women in his critique of racist thinking, as a case in point. Because the patriarchal bias has been contested in English, I have seen fit, where possible, to include it in the translation. The purpose is not to produce a literal translation, but a work in English that expresses what the work in French expresses as closely as possible. I distinguish three cases of male-biased language in Memmi's text and adopt different strategies for dealing with each.

The first is where Memmi attributes or deploys the male gender in his discussion of racist thinking or behavior. In those cases, I have usually left it as it is, because I agree with Memmi that patriarchal thinking is quite akin in form and structure to racism as he is presenting it, and to which the male-biased language makes veiled reference. In cases where he refers to racist thinking that, it should be recognized, certainly includes women as well, I have sought to neutralize the male bias of the reference.

The second case is a philosophical use of the male gender that is correctable through modifications in the translation, without disrupting the flow of Memmi's ideas. In those cases, I have attempted to translate his text into gender-neutral language.

The third case is where such a translation into gender-neutral language would either be disruptive of the flow of Memmi's ideas, or where these ideas themselves are deeply embedded in a historico-ethical terminology that is patriarchal. In some cases, the sense of male bias appears inescapable in terms of the philosophical language in which it has historically been couched; for instance, when it appears immersed in generalities about the human that devolve from eighteenth- or nineteenth-century patriarchal ideology. In those cases, I have left the language in its male-biased form, while noting it through diacritical reference.—Trans.]

4. [The Midi and Nord are regions of France. The "Midi" is the southern region, which stretches from the Pyrenees mountains to the Italian border on the east. "Nord" is the uppermost corner of France, bordered by the English Channel and Belgium on the north, and the Ardennes to the southeast. "Nord" is also the name of one of the departments (administrative unit, like a "state" in the United States) in that region. "Provence" is the easternmost province in the Midi, abutting Italy; Nice is its major city.—Trans.]

5. I have already described this effect as a "cultural concentration" in Albert Memmi, *Portrait of a Jew,* trans. Elisabeth Abbott (New York: Orion Press, 1962); originally published as *Portrait d'un Juif* (Paris: Gallimard, 1962).

6. [The Maghreb is that region of northern Africa that stretches from the Atlas mountains on the Atlantic coast in Morocco to Lybia in the east. Its original population was Berber. It was invaded and settled by Arab peoples (Moors) during their expansion across Africa and into Spain in the eighth century, and it was mainly colonized by France in the eighteenth and nineteenth centuries.—Trans.]

7. [Bretons are the people of Bretagne, the westernmost region of France, reaching out into the Atlantic. They have an ancient dialect peculiar to that region and have moved at different times for autonomy. Alsatians are the people of Alsace (see note 13).—Trans.]

8. [Saracen is a general name given to the Arabs of

the Middle East during the Crusades of the Middle Ages. It is now an archaic term.—Trans.]

9. See, for example, the brilliant and lucid discussions of Professor Jean Bernard.

10. [The assumption of entitlement is what empowered the Bakke case and constitutes the ideological core of the charge of reverse racism. As Cheryl Harris argues, the court, in ordering Bakke admitted to medical school, assumed that his expectation of a certain privilege was valid, and that African-Americans, in seeking remediation for past constraint and discrimination, were limited by the extent of infringement on such expectations. If "merit" is a constructed idea, and hence not objectively determinable, in limiting its consideration of "merit" to Bakke's grade point average and MCAT scores, the court was in effect assuming a particular and partisan definition of "merit," to which they then held the medical school, to Bakke's favor.

The Supreme Court's rejection of affirmative action programs on the grounds that race-conscious remedial measures are unconstitutional under the Equal Protection Clause of the Fourteenth Amendment—the very constitutional measure designed to guarantee equality for Blacks—is based on the court's chronic refusal to dismantle the institutional protection of benefits for Whites that have been based on white supremacy and maintained at the expense of Blacks. As a result, the parameters of appropriate remedies are not dictated by the scope of the injury to the subjugated but by the extent of the infringement on settled expectations of Whites. Cheryl Harris, "Whiteness as Property," *Harvard Law Review,* vol. 106:1707–1791 (1993): pp. 1766–73.—Trans.]

11. Sartre has noted, for anti-Semitism, that it is a "passion," which is to say that one undergoes it rather than enacts it. See Jean-Paul Sartre, *Anti-Semite and Jew,* trans. George J. Becker (New York: Schocken Books, 1976); originally published as *Réflexions sur la question juive* (Paris: P. Morihien, 1946). [This can be seen in the etymology of the term *passion.* Passion relates to *passive* in the same way that *action* relates to *active.* Sartre's point is that one is passive in the face of a passion, which takes one over, as if it were a current of water in which one can only drift.—Trans.]

12. Some authors, for instance, Maxime Rodinson and François de Fontette, have reproached my definition for being too broad: "The classical definition of racism by Albert Memmi . . . is inconvenient in not being sufficiently definitive." What is not seen here is the impossibility of comprehensively grasping each form without contextualizing it in a very general structure. Furthermore, the distinction I make between racism and heterophobia is precisely what makes possible a response to the duality between a narrow view and a broad view. Cf. François de Fontette, *Le racisme* (Paris: Presses Universitaires de France, 1975); Maxime Rodinson, "Racisme, ethnisme, xénophobie," in *Dictionnaire du savoir moderne*. In addition, see *Racisme et société, ouvrage collectif redigé sous la direction de Patrice de Comarmond et de Claude Duchet, avec la participation de Marc-André Bloch, Patrice de Comarmond, Michele Duchet, Arnaud Durban, et al.* (Paris: Maspero, 1969).

13. [Alsace-Lorraine is the northeastern corner of France. The two provinces named, which constitute this region, have been the rope in a tug of war between France and Germany since the early nineteenth century. The region was at the center of Charlemagne's empire in the ninth century, and it was incorporated as one of the "Germanies" under the Holy Roman Empire until the Thirty Years' War (1618–48). In the Treaty of Westphalia (1648), the region was given to France. It was then ceded to Germany after the Franco-Prussian War of 1870, which France lost. Then, it was ceded to France again in 1919, after the First World War, which Germany lost. It was taken by Germany in 1940 at the beginning of the Second World War, and retaken by France in 1945, at the end of it. The population of the region has found things to dislike in both nations, and there have been recurrent movements for regional autonomy. The Alsatian language is a German dialect.—Trans.]

14. [The "rumor of Orleans" was a mass hysteria event that took place in the city of Orleans, just south of Paris, during May and June 1969. Some Jewish clothing-store owners were accused of drugging women with chloroform in the stores' fitting rooms, imprisoning them in the basement, and then selling them into prostitution, as a kind of white slave trade. The story

apparently began among some teenagers but soon spread to the rest of the city. No women had been reported missing, but the rumor spread anyway. Mobs formed outside the stores in question, and a general hatred of all Jews was expressed. The MRAP, of which Memmi speaks in this book, and the LICA (Ligue international contre le racisme et l'antisémitisme) became involved and played a role in defusing the situation. After the confrontation, the situation diminished to the rumor stage, and from there into oblivion. The entire cycle took about two months. See Edgar Morin, *Rumour in Orleans,* in collaboration with Bernard Paillard et al., trans. Peter Green (New York: Pantheon Books, 1971); originally published as *La Rumeur d'Orléans,* with Bernard Paillard, Evelyne Burguière, Claude Capulier, Suzanne de Lusignan, et al. (Paris: Editions du Seuil, 1969).—Trans.]

15. For a sociological perspective on these questions, see the excellent work of Michel Wieviorka, *L'espace du racisme* (Paris: Editions de Seuil, 1991).

16. [Alphonse Toussenel was a follower of Charles Fourier. Both men were anti-Semitic and socialist. Fourier felt that the merchant class was the main evil, that Jews constituted the core of the merchant class, and that therefore they were an evil race. Toussenel carried this one step further. For him, the Jews were usurers, merchants, anti-Christian, and finally Protestant in being predators and libertines. Toussenel was himself Catholic. He later became disaffected from the socialist movement and became a naturalist of some repute. See Robert F. Byrnes, *Antisemitism in Modern France,* vol. 1 (New Brunswick: Rutgers University Press, 1950); Stephen Wilson, *Ideology and Experience* (Rutherford: Fairleigh Dickinson University Press, 1982).—Trans.]

17. Cf. Albert Memmi, *Dependence: A Sketch for a Portrait of the Dependent,* trans. Philip A. Facey (Boston: Beacon Press, 1984); originally published as *La dépendance: esquisse pour un portrait du dépendant* (Paris: Gallimard, 1979).

18. Cf. Albert Memmi, *The Colonizer and the Colonized,* trans. Howard Greenfield, with an introduction by Jean-Paul Sartre and an afterword by Susan Gilson Miller (Boston: Beacon Press, 1991); originally published as *Portrait du colonisé,*

précédé de portrait du colonisateur: et d'une préface de Jean-Paul Sartre (Paris: Corréa, 1957).

19. [The French expression is *racisme à rebours,* literally, "reverse racism," but I translate it as "inverted racism" instead because "reverse racism" has been given a specific political meaning in the United States. In the unfolding of affirmative action programs to alleviate the effects of past discrimination, a certain preferential treatment has been necessary, but which signifies to many Whites that their privilege no longer holds the weight it used to, and they have charged "reverse racism." Thus, the term *reverse racism* refers to a defense of former modes of discrimination against non-whites. But Memmi is talking about a person or group establishing cultural or historical preferences for themselves out of their own being in the world, which, if they sought to impose that as an aesthetic standard on others, would constitute an inversion of the aesthetic and ethical impositions of contemporary racism. We see examples of the kind of domain Memmi is talking about in the fashion industry, where a certain thinness of body type has led to the exclusion of many people from the attention of fashion standards. These standards have caused some overweight people to lose their jobs because of how they looked (not to mention attendant psychological dysfunctions, such as anorexia and bulimia). The establishment of such norms does not constitute racism, but it is one of the procedures that lie at the core of all racist structures.—Trans.]

20. By *différence,* it goes without saying, I am referring to a trait differential and not to its concrete being or actual substantiality; in any case, it is wiser to employ the plural: *différences.*

21. Albert Memmi, *A Contre-courants,* illustrations by Michel Ciardi (Paris: Nouvel Objet, 1993).

22. [The Jacobins were the radicals of the French Revolution, who sought the most complete dismantling of the old feudal aristocratic structure in the name of the equality of "man." They introduced the Declaration of the Rights of Man into the revolutionary process. In attempting to unify France under the republic, the revolution ended up fighting not only the aristocracy, many of whom had fled to England as a base of counterrevolutionary

operations, but local armies of peasants and former serfs who resisted the revolution in the name of loyalty to that same nobility. This conflict reached its most critical level in the province of Vendée, in western France. Victor Hugo's novel *Ninety-Three* is a brilliant portrait of the human issues involved in that struggle.—Trans.]

23. The texts to which I refer are not numerous. One work of interest is Rudolph Maurice Loewenstein, *Christians and Jews: A Psychoanalytic Study*, trans. Vera Damman (New York: International Universities Press, 1952); originally published as *Psychanalyse de l'antisémitisme* (Paris, 1950). See also Jacques Hassoun, "Approaches psychanalytique du problème du racisme," in *Colloque de Cerisy sur le racisme* (1975); Albert Jacquard and J.-B. Pontalis, "Une tête qui ne revient pas," interview in *Le Genre Humain* 11 (1984–85).

24. [This type of realization initiated the contemporary critique of humanism, now associated with poststructuralist thought. In the process of anti-colonial struggle, many people came to realize that the human being that Western humanism spoke about was the White European human being, and that humanism had imposed it as an ideological concept, derived from a European cultural background, on other cultures that were different. The purpose of the critique of humanism was not to "throw humanism out," as some of its detractors have claimed, but to reveal its limits and biases, and thus to open the notion of the humane, which humanism had sought to place in the center of human activity, to a multiplicity of nonimpositional contexts.—Trans.]

25. On the importance of ideology for racism, see the works of Colette Guillaumin, in particular *L'idéologie raciste: Genèse et langage actuel* (La Haye: Mouton, 1972).

26. [This is a question that Frantz Fanon addresses in *The Wretched of the Earth*—that is, the dislocating and unbalancing psychological effects of colonialism and its brutality, and what the process of national liberation, in its many forms, offered as practical therapy—and perhaps, he theorized, the only practical therapy—for the psychological ills suffered by the colonized. Frantz Fanon, *The Wretched of the Earth,* preface by Jean-Paul

Sartre, trans. Constance Farrington (New York: Grove Press, 1965); originally published as *Les damnés de la terre,* preface by Jean-Paul Sartre (Paris: Maspero, 1961).—Trans.]

27. On "the return of the pendulum," see my essay by that name in Albert Memmi, *Dominated Man: Notes toward a Portrait* (Boston: Beacon Press, 1969); originally published as *L'Homme dominé* (Paris: Gallimard, 1968).

28. [I leave these terms for degrees of "racial mixture" in French, since the English equivalents have become archaic and do not need to be resurrected here.—Trans.]

29. I have developed this notion of "costs to be paid" for all such "services rendered" in my article "Dependence," in "Le Prix de la Santé," *Perspective et santé publique* (December 1982).

30. Like many, Jews included, I have not written "holocaust" because I think it is already understood as the meaning of the genocide of the Jews. To use it also suggests, however, more or less unconsciously, that the Jews were the chosen victims, the scapegoats, for an expiatory sacrifice. For many Jews, its use often reflects an interiorization, an acceptance, of that accusation, which is what makes the machinery of the scapegoat work in the first place.

At the moment of drafting this note, a similar remark fell beneath my eyes in Bruno Bettelheim's book, *Surviving, and Other Essays* (New York: Knopf, 1979).

31. For a historical view of anti-Semitism, beyond the works of Leon Poliakov, there are several histories of the Jewish people. See, in particular, Heinrich Graetz, *History of the Jews* (Philadelphia: Jewish Publication Society, 1891); Salo Wittmeyer Baron, *A Social and Religious History of the Jews* (New York: Columbia University Press, 1952); Simon Dubnow, *History of the Jews,* trans. Moshe Spiegel (South Brunswick: Yoseloff, 1967).

On the Roman period and the beginning of Christianity, Jules Isaac has gotten to the core of it. See Jules Isaac, *Jesus and Israel,* edited and with a foreword by Claire Huchet Bishop, trans. Sally Gran (New York: Holt, Rinehart and Winston,

1971); also, *Genèse de l'antisémitisme; Essai historique* (Paris: Calmann-Levy, 1956).

32. Gobineau would have done better to title his book "Essay on the Differences . . . ," which more closely corresponds to his content, rather than "Essay on the Inequalities." But it is true that for him, as for his followers, difference justifies inequality.

33. Bernard Lazare, *Antisemitism: Its History and Causes* (London: Britons Publishing, 1967); originally published as *L'Antisémitisme: Son histoire et ses causes* (Paris: Editions Léon Chailley, 1894).

34. [Medina is an oasis and city in Saudi Arabia, the second most sacred city of Islam after Mecca. Mohammed traveled from Mecca to Medina in 622, at which time it was a small settlement inhabited by Jews who had fled Palestine. Mohammed seized the town from them and built it into the capital city of the Islamic state, the source from which the expansion of Islam across Asia and North Africa originated.—Trans.]

35. On the topic of Jewish-Arab relations, we might add that over the past few years, an unexpected mode of ostracism has appeared in the very interior of Jewish communities, on the part of European (Ashkenazi) Jews toward Asian (Sephardic) Jews. The Asian Jews complain bitterly, and not without reason, of being discriminated against, even in Israel. Some might consider their alarm to be excessive, but it can't be denied that the rise to power by the Western Jews has led them, as elsewhere, to disparage and discriminate against the Sephardic Jews. A critical pursuit of this phenomenon would be interesting since it is unfolding before our eyes. The Jews of the Mediterranean have universally shared the historic eclipse that others of the Mediterranean have also suffered. With the end of colonization and the rise of a new national independence, they begin to raise their head. Naturally, the inevitable countermyths appear: a magnified sense of folklore, cuisine, and music, with an avid search for all that could heighten the collective consciousness. I have now heard it claimed, in Israel, that the Asian Jews are taking power, meaning it is now their turn (the return of the pendulum).

36. [The Marranos were Jews living in Spain during

the fourteenth and fifteenth centuries who had converted to Christianity under duress and continued to practice Judaism in secret. This was the time of the *Reconquista,* the war against the Moors who had occupied Spain for the previous six hundred years. In 1492, the Moors were defeated and driven out by the Christians under Ferdinand and Isabel. From the middle of the fourteenth century until that time, there were continual attacks against the Jews, and many converted to Christianity to escape persecution, rather than go into exile. Not all continued to practice the Jewish religion in secret, but for the Catholic church of the time, if some did, then all were suspect of doing so. Thus, the term Marrano, which originally referred only to those converts who continued to practice Judaism in secret, came to refer to all the Jewish converts. It was ostensibly to root out the Marranos, but also, as Memmi says, to consolidate elite Christian control of the state, that the Spanish Inquisition was begun in 1478. There had been riots against the Jews in 1473 in Cordova, which spread to the rest of Spain. To establish order and gain control of the anti-Semitic sentiment, the Christian government induced Pope Sixtus IV to authorize the Inquisition, which then lasted until the mid-1800s. Tens of thousands of Jews were killed during the first decades of the Inquisition, leading up to their expulsion from Spain in 1492, along with the Moors.—Trans.]

37. See Paul Hassan Maucorps, *Les Français et le racisme,* with Albert Memmi and Jean-Francis Held, from a survey taken among anti-racists; it is written in cooperation with the "Mouvement contre le racisme, l'antisémitisme et pour la paix" (MRAP) (Paris: Payot, 1965).

38. [It is worth noting that the feminist movement has produced a critique of the "pill." It recognizes that the birth control pill has been a mixed blessing. There are many shortcomings: (1) it distorts a woman's metabolism and hormonal balance; (2) it signifies to men that the women using the pill are "available" for a sexual relation, and therefore feeds into the patriarchal assumption that a man has entitlement to and can expect a relation with a woman; and (3) it represents the traditional hierarchy by which the social problem of offspring is located in the personhood and body of a woman, not that of a man or in the arena of social

and political responsibility. The benefits of the pill were political, as a first step (at the time it was introduced) toward a recognition and a possibility of what it would look like to be free of the biological straitjacket imposed on women by patriarchy. The pill was not an answer to the straitjacket; a critique of the straitjacket as a social construct that justified misplacing the responsibility of childbearing wholly on the individual woman, and thus erasing all social responsibility, has still to be done. To transform that justification and the alibi it manifests, union struggles, more volumes of argument, and more political activity will be necessary. Cf. Catharine A. MacKinnon, *Feminism Unmodified* (Cambridge: Harvard University Press, 1987).—Trans.]

39. [This point is analyzed in great depth by Gayatri Spivak in her often-misunderstood essay "Can the Subaltern Speak?" In that essay, she argues that not only are the oppressed given a deaf ear and that what they have to say is ignored, ridiculed, or trivialized, but most important, they are already spoken for by the oppressor, the ruling class or caste. Words are already put in the subaltern's mouth, so that what she or he says is heard as being what has been already said for her or him, and not what is in fact said. Thus, every avenue of self-expression, self-affirmation, and self-defense for the subaltern is closed. Gayatri Spivak, "Can the Subaltern Speak?" in *Marxism and the Interpretation of Culture*, Larry Grossman and Cary Nelson, eds. (Urbana: University of Illinois Press, 1988).—Trans.]

40. I have already dealt with the notion of "minority" elsewhere. I would reiterate here that it is not simply a demographic concept. One can be minoritized in many ways. On the whole, women and the colonized, though demographically more numerous than those who dominate them, represent cases of such minoritization. Black Americans and Jews are doubly minoritary.

41. [Memmi is being metaphoric here, but he has his finger on a significant difference between France and the United States on this question. In France, the subject of race is more often thought through in philosophical terms; in the United States, the invention of race has always involved and relied on juridical enactment. The evolution of slavery, the disenfranchisements of Jim Crow, the administrative disregard of lynching and lynch law, and

the contemporary criminalization of minorities produced by massive arrest and imprisonment patterns are all examples of a juridical if not a judicial involvement in the constructions of racism in the United States. Part of the structure of law suggests why the juridical is critical to the establishment of racism and race. Law as a social institution incarnates the very structure of nonreciprocity. Though the individual law, through the judge, can judge the individual person, the individual person cannot judge the individual law. If the "jury of one's peers" was to be the community-law interface, it has now to accept the law and participate only in judging the accused. For reciprocity to be possible, a juridical procedure based on dialogue and community involvement, rather than an adversarial contest in a hermetic specialized context, would have to be developed. And a narrative would have to become a permissible response to a question that now calls for only a yes or no answer. In being politically invented, imposed, and institutionally nonreciprocal, the law actually represents an analogue model of racism.—Trans.]

DEFINITION

1. *Le Nef,* special double issue on racism, 19–20 (1964): 41–47. [*Le Nef* is a journal of social and political commentary and analysis, combining critical theories with a sociological approach.—Trans.]

2. [We have, of course, seen this kind of illogical reasoning used again and again in various war efforts. There is, for instance, the notion of a "preventive reaction strike," which gained currency during the war in Vietnam. See Felix Greene, *The Enemy: What Every American Should Know about Imperialism* (New York: Vintage Books, 1971). This was one of many euphemisms for the various military operations against the population of three Southeast Asian countries. Aside from the offensiveness of both the idea and the military operation it named, the structure of thought Memmi is addressing could perhaps be what made it seem intelligible to the population of the United States as a rhetorical expression. Nicaragua was a similar case. The United States

engaged in military operations against that country, through a proxy army known as the "Contras," and when Nicaragua sought to defend itself against those operations, it was labeled "aggressive," and the military operations against it were augmented. The iconic example is the rule written into the structures of both slavery and Jim Crow, which made it a punishable crime, at times a felony, for a Black person to defend himself or herself against any aggression whatsoever by a White person. Obviously, such a law wholly authorized the rape of any Black woman by a White man. Not only was her defense to be considered criminal and hence aggressive, but if she could not legally reject his attentions, then the White man's assault was not an assault. For a further account of the history of the "defensive reaction strike," and the notion of defense as aggression as it emerged in the original colonies, see Dee Alexander Brown, *Bury My Heart at Wounded Knee* (New York: Washington Square Press, 1981).—Trans.]

3. [Interestingly enough, in this era of corporate globalization, the French term Memmi uses here is *globalization,* which I have translated as "generalization," though the verb *globalizer* is more active than the English verb "to generalize." The French term implies a process of bringing together into a whole, a unification of elements, whereas the English term connotes an operation of logic, of reasoning from particular cases to a general idea. In mathematics, this logical process is known as "induction." In the discourse of racism or bigotry, rather than reason from the particular to the general, there is an imposition of the general on the particular. As Memmi has pointed out, racism contains an ideological dimension; one of the ways ideology expresses itself is in that moment of imposition that parallels the process of induction without bothering to understand that induction is not a possible procedure when it comes to people (as I discuss in the Introduction to this book). Its impossibility does not, however, stop the bigot, who uses the general against the particular in order to use the particular to confirm the general.—Trans.]

4. Sometimes, I leave the term *valuation* unmodified by either of the adjectives "generalized" or "ultimate," because I am mainly concerned with the nature of the valuation.

5. [I have left all these derogatory terms in French,

since they are derogatory terms in French, though some of them may correspond to derogatory terms in English. But the correspondence does not need to be explicated, because, I would argue, derogatory terms are not signifiers, that is, signs with specific meanings that can be translated. They are, instead, acts of assault based on discourses of denigration that give them the power to act with a certain pre-established injuriousness. For this reason derogatory terms are unanswerable in language; they do not exist in language but rather in the experiential contexts of modes of domination and oppression. Thus, there is nothing to translate; their meaning lies in their use. Indeed, one could say that they are always already translated, since all derogatory terms have the same non-meaning and the same function as their essential meaning, that is, as forms of assault whose purpose is to hurt and reduce in status.—Trans.]

6. [See, on this point, the writing of Ida B. Wells. Her descriptions and analyses of lynchings that occurred during the 1890s in the United States bear out Memmi's account. Wells probes the way preparatory nullifications of African-Americans, the fragility of the racial relations whose stasis could so easily be broken by a rumor or a newspaper editorial, the indifference as to which African-American to attack, and the need to destroy a member of the group of African-Americans all serve both as ends in themselves and, as Wells argues, an extended process of disenfranchisement.

Today, the massive incarceration of Black people is a contemporary version of the partial physical destruction that Memmi is focusing on. It is a version of the idea of holding against the victim what one does to him or her. On all of these issues, see Daniel Jonah Goldhagen, *Hitler's Willing Executioners: Ordinary Germans and the Holocaust* (New York: Knopf, 1996), for a discussion of how similar processes unfolded in Germany before and during the reign of the Nazis.—Trans.]

7. At the same time, one could envisage even more varied meanings; it does not seem restricted in use. Do we not say, "he belongs to a race of artisans who are fast disappearing" or "politicians are a peculiar race"? Why not? It simply requires that one be fully aware that one is approaching closer and closer to

metaphor, or to catch-all expressions, as, for example, in "anti-cop racism."

8. Does this mean giving up the term *racism*? I thought of it for a moment. A conference was held in Paris in 1992, to which I was invited, whose task was to respond to this question. All things considered, I think that such semantic battles are a waste of time. Words have a history of their own. What is important is to be as clear as possible about one's meanings and definitions.

TREATMENT

1. [Hannah Arendt, *Eichmann in Jerusalem: A Report on the Banality of Evil* (New York: Viking Press, 1963).—Trans.]

2. [Christopher R. Browning, *Ordinary Men: Reserve Police Battalion 101 and the Final Solution in Poland* (New York: HarperCollins, 1992).—Trans.]

3. [Raul Hilberg, *The Destruction of the European Jews* (New York: Holmes and Meier, 1985); *Documents of Destruction: Germany and Jewry, 1933–1945*, edited with commentary by Raul Hilberg (Chicago: Quadrangle Books, 1971); Raul Hilberg, *Perpetrators, Victims, Bystanders: The Jewish Catastrophe, 1933–1945* (New York: Aaron Asher Books, 1992). See also Robert Jay Lifton, *The Nazi Doctors: Medical Killing and the Psychology of Genocide* (New York: Basic Books, 1986). Also, Goldhagen, *Hitler's Willing Executioners.*—Trans.]

4. Albert Memmi, "Must It Be Spoken Of?" in *Evidences*, September–October 1961. After a television program devoted to the issue of racism, the producers entrusted me with the correspondence from the viewers in order to make a report for this journal.

5. [The phenomenon of the Gypsy is not alien to the United States. The Gypsies in Europe are largely migratory; having been forced to emigrate from their original homeland in India, they move about to keep in touch with one another and to renew acquaintances. But they are also driven from places of congregation

by an anti-Gypsy hostility in many locales. In their role of scapegoat, they are used by local inhabitants to construct a cross-class social cohesiveness. This relation is given political sanction through legal enactment and police action against the Gypsies, which taints them as criminal. For a very personal and insightful view of the Gypsies in Europe from their side, see Jan Yoors, *The Gypsies*.

In the United States, migratory labor populations function analogously. Three large migratory regions exist: through California, from south to north, largely Mexican and Filipino; from Texas north through the central states to Chicago and Minnesota, harvesting wheat and other grains, largely Mexican and Black; and from Florida, picking fruit and vegetables, up through the Carolinas and Kentucky into Ohio and Michigan, largely Black and Caribbean. There are some White laborers in these migratory labor forces, but not many, though during the Depression they constituted the majority. On the East Coast, these laborers are housed in labor camps and discouraged from going into neighboring towns. They are told that the population is hostile, and when they go into town, they are arrested by the police under suspicion of drunkenness and thievery. The police do not act as a buffer between them and local populations but rather as the proxy for a local hostility that may or may not exist. Thus, confined to camps and unable to make their own way, they are forced to buy goods at company stores that charge higher prices and loan money at exorbitant rates. Migratory labor becomes a form of semi-slavery. Yet the migratory laborers play a direct economic role, more so than the Gypsies in Europe. Rather than scapegoats, they serve to construct a social cross-class cohesiveness by inhabiting the bottom layer. They manifest an alternate form of class differentiation, one between themselves and all others in solidarity against them. It is in this sense that White solidarity has traditionally been substituted for class difference, implying an absorption of class interest into what amounts to White collaboration. This is what kept the South non-union for so long. See Roediger, *The Wages of Whiteness* (New York: Verso, 1991), and Saxton, *The Indispensable Enemy* (Berkeley: University of California Press, 1971). For the tip of the iceberg concerning migratory labor camps on the East Coast, see the *New York Times*,

April 17, 1989; October 31, 1989; June 24, 1990 (Long Island edition); February 8, 1992; September 1, 1992.—Trans.]

6. A well-known man of letters, M. Fabre-Luce, in the pages of *Figaro,* recommended that the Jews become transparent. Why does he not become transparent himself, he who is still trying, even now, to defend the Vichy government? Clearly, he is part of the majority. But why, if not by virtue of the law that "might makes right," can the majority live as they like, and not the minorities?

7. [In a note to the 1994 edition of this book, Memmi adds here: *Unfortunately, this is no longer the case.*—Trans.]

8. The substance of these ideas is developed in an article that serves as the conclusion for the book *Les Français et le racisme.*

9. See Memmi, *Portrait of a Jew,* especially the first part of chapter 6.

10. [It is the explicit logic of racist thinking to hold the victim responsible for what is done to him or her. It was the logic of the anti-immigrant movement that campaigned for Proposition 187; it is the logic of minoritization, holding an excluded group responsible for having "special minority interests" that are only that group's response to having been excluded and rendered a minority. See William Ryan, *Blaming the Victim* (New York: Vintage, 1976).—Trans.]

11. See Memmi, *A Contre-courants,* in which I denounce certain contemporary myths, while fully recognizing which social needs they are responding to.

12. Denis Diderot, *Supplément au Voyage de Bougainville* (Geneva: Librarie Droz, 1955). It is a playful lesson in cultural relativism to remind the racist thinker of the philosophers of the eighteenth century.

13. [John Howard Griffin, *Black Like Me,* updated and with a new epilogue by the author (New York: New American Library, 1976).—Trans.]

14. [What could be added, in this regard, is the issue of organization around racist opinion. Social organizations to further racist opinion are, by their very existence, already beyond

mere opinion, but not yet necessarily at the point of action or attack. There are many examples in the United States (e.g., the White Citizens Councils, the militias, the Whites-only clubs and membership bars, country clubs, and so on). Only recently have they begun to appear in France, the primary example being Le Pen's right-wing party, the "Action National." Many clubs and militias claim not to discriminate, but Black people find the atmosphere particularly unwelcoming. Exclusion should be considered an action; it goes beyond opinion; this would include redlining by the finance industry. And the same goes for derogatory speech (see note 5 of "Definition" in this book). Finally, there are laws, such as the Jim Crow laws, that are also neither opinion nor action but valorize the racist action of citizens.—Trans.]

15. See Albert Memmi, *Agar, un roman* (Paris: Corréa, 1955).

16. Pierre-André Taguieff, *La force du préjugé: essai sur le racisme et ses doubles* (Paris: La Decouverte, 1988). Those interested in this essentially rhetorical polemic can consult the works of Paul Yonnet. This author, provoked by the excesses of certain anti-racists, has essentially set racism and anti-racism back to back. *Le Monde* [the newspaper of record in France, comparable to the *New York Times*], devoted a page to this quarrel, and to the relation between this critique of anti-racism and the revisionist maneuvers of the "new right." [In France, the term *revisionist* has a specific meaning; it refers to a movement of political thinkers and historians to deny the reports of Nazi atrocities and in particular, of the death camps and the campaign to exterminate the Jews.—Trans.]

One might consult as well the courageous journal of Lyon, *Le Croquant* (ed., Michel Cornaton), 13 and 14 (1993).

17. Let me take this occasion to say something on the question of humanism. Humanism has been subjected to some harsh critique over the past few decades. I have myself at times been party to this. Some important distinctions need to be made.

The fascists violently condemn and despise humanism because they reject the image of the human being that it proposes.

Our disagreement with it has, of course, a totally

different significance; we regret that, in its generous spirit toward the universal human, toward fraternity based on reason, toward a common denominator for all people, the humanists succeed in neglecting some very real, specific, and concrete problems concerning specific people. The fact that some people are in difficult historical situations, such as the victims of colonization, or Black people confronting White racism, is not taken into account. Because of this, humanism runs the risk of becoming a philosophy of alibi, as in the pretended civilizing "mission" of colonialism. That said, however, I do not refuse the humanist ideal, but it still remains to be promoted. That is, it is still up ahead of us, and not behind. Cf. Memmi, *A Contre-courants,* in particular the article "Humanisme."

18. See Memmi, "La Loi Commune," in *Tribune de Genève,* September 18, 1993.

19. This is, as we have seen, one of the difficulties of the affirmation of difference, as legitimate as that may be otherwise.

20. [The events in Poland to which Memmi refers occurred in 1970. There had been unrest in the wake of student strikes in 1968 in solidarity with Prague. In December 1970, the government announced price increases on food and other commodities. There was an immediate eruption of strikes and demonstrations in Gdansk, centered around the shipyards there. Crowds attacked the Communist Party headquarters in the city and set it on fire. The police opened fire on the crowds, and many were killed. The next day, the shipyards were struck in Gdynia, and Gdansk went on general strike. The strikes spread to Slupsk, Elblag, and finally to Szczecin. In Gdansk there was fighting between the strikers and the police, and both suffered many casualties. The demands of the workers were mainly a recognition of worker shop committees to run the shipyards and factories, prosecution of those who did the shooting, and a rescinding of the price increases. Gomulka was removed as head of Poland, and Gierek took his place. See Neal Ascherson, *The Polish August: The Self-Limiting Revolution* (New York: Penguin, 1981), and Jakub Karpinski, *Countdown: The Polish Upheavals of 1956, 1968, 1970, 1976, 1980,* trans. Olga Amsterdamska and Gene Moore (New York: Karz-Cohl, 1988). Andrzej Wajda then incorporated these events into his two highly

political films of that period, *Man of Marble* and *Man of Iron*. See Janina Falkowska, *The Political Films of Andrzej Wajda: Dialogism in "Man of Marble," "Man of Iron," and "Danton."*—Trans.]

21. It is Aime Césaire who pointed out the correspondence between social hierarchy and this scale of skin colors. Aime Césaire, *Notebook of a Return to My Native Land*, trans. Mireille Rosello with Annie Pritchard, introduction by Mireille Rosello (Newcastle-on-Tyne: Bloodaxe Books, 1995); originally published as *Cahier d'un retour au pays natal* (Paris: Presence Africaine, 1983).

22. R. Etiemble, *La péché vraiment capital* (Paris: Gallimard, 1957).

"AN ATTEMPT AT A DEFINITION"

1. If further summary were necessary, I would say that racism seems to me to include three essential elements: insisting on a difference, putting it to mythical use, and the convenience of such use.

2. Or even at times a genuine inadequacy. Of course, the racist, far from viewing it as a result of the oppression to which he himself subjects his victim or at least of the objective conditions that the victim is made to endure, holds that inadequacy against him, as if it were a defect or flaw. Examples are the technical unpreparedness of the colonized that is the result of colonization, and the high rate of absenteeism among working women, the result of their family duties.

3. I have run into a good deal of argument over this phrase, "placing a value on the difference." Here, of course, it has the strict meaning of assigning either a negative or a positive value.

4. See, in *The Colonizer and the Colonized*, the notion of the "Negro complex," which also includes this seesaw movement, both complementary and contradictory.

5. Yet the fact of an individual motivation does not cancel out the mediation of the social factor, which I consider crucial in any racist process. Individual motivation does not

become genuine racism until it is filtered through the culture and the ideologies of a group. In the prevailing stereotypes it seeks and finds the explanation of its own uneasiness, which is then turned into racism. The individual racist actually discovers discrimination all about him—in his education and his culture—as a potential mental attitude, and he adopts it when he feels the need to do so. The intermediary of society is felt on two levels: that of the victim, as member of a guilty and defective group, and that of the accuser, representative of a normal and healthy group.

6. See the conclusions reached in *The Colonizer and the Colonized* and *Portrait of a Jew.* The colonized should not, any more than the Jew or the Black, be unfaithful to himself or use camouflage in order to disarm his prejudiced adversaries. He should insist on being accepted as he is, differences and all.

WHAT IS RACISM?

1. This is not the way the excellent *Dictionary* of Bescherelle thinks of the matter. For him, *race* comes not from *ratio* (chronological order) but from *radix,* which signifies lines of descent, lineage, or "root," i.e., those who belong to the same family. Its usage seems to have amalgamated the two meanings in the same term.

2. [Memmi's reference to the seventeenth century is probably a misprint. Both Eric Williams and Daniel Mannix argue that the eighteenth century was the period of greatest slave trade activity—which is also when Montesquieu wrote. It was, however, the most important industry in the Atlantic economy during the seventeenth century. Indeed, much of English and U.S. industrialization was based on profit accumulation from the slave trade. It is worth noting that the slave trade did not end with its prohibition at the beginning of the nineteenth century. Cf. Daniel Mannix, *Black Cargoes: A History of the Atlantic Slave Trade* (New York: Viking Press, 1962); Eric Eustace Williams, *Capitalism and Slavery,* with a new introduction by Colin A. Palmer (Chapel Hill: University of North Carolina Press, 1994).—Trans.]

3. There are those who conclude, perhaps a bit too

hastily, that biological racism originated during the Enlightenment. Though the development of the biological sciences was of use to racism, the philosophers of that time, both French and English, were on the whole initiators of freedom of thought and of social justice. The French revolutionaries, despite the hesitations of some among them, abolished slavery—something the Vatican, for example, could not bring itself even to condemn until 1889.

ALBERT MEMMI
was born and raised in Tunis, Tunisia, and lives in Paris. A novelist and critic, he has written extensively on colonialism, anti-Semitism, and racism. His books include *The Colonizer and the Colonized, Dominated Man,* and *The Pillar of Salt*. He is professor emeritus of sociology at the University of Paris, Nanterre.

STEVE MARTINOT
has worked as an activist in the anti-racist and anti-war movements. He recently received a Ph.D. in literature from the University of California, Santa Cruz.

KWAME ANTHONY APPIAH
is professor of Afro-American studies and philosophy at Harvard University. He is the author of many works, including *Color Conscious: The Political Morality of Race* (with Amy Gutman). He coedited the recently published *Perseus Africana Encyclopedia* with Henry Louis Gates Jr.